Number 10

Number 10

The Private Lives of Six Prime Ministers

TERENCE FEELY

SIDGWICK & JACKSON
LONDON

Number 10 Yorkshire Television Production Credits:
Creator & Writer of the Series: Terence Feely
Executive Producer: David Cunliffe
Producer: Margaret Bottomley
Directors:
Herbert Wise
John Glenister
David Cunliffe
David Reynolds
Designers:
Roger Andrews
with
Jeremy Bear
David Crozier
Stills Photographer: Brian Cleasby

First published in Great Britain in 1982
by Sidgwick & Jackson Limited
Reprinted February 1983
Copyright © Serprocor Establishment
Stills copyright © YTV 1982

ISBN 0-283-98893-2

Printed in Great Britain by
R. J. Acford, Chichester, Sussex
for Sidgwick & Jackson Limited
1 Tavistock Chambers, Bloomsbury Way
London WC1A 2SG

To my wife, Elizabeth

Contents

Picture Acknowledgements

The illustration on page 26 is reproduced by gracious permission of H.M. the Queen and the illustrations on pages 65, 67, 77 and 79 by courtesy of His Grace the Duke of Wellington. Other photographs and illustrations were supplied or are reproduced by kind permission of the following: Bodleian Library: 19; British Library: 18, 30, 38, 55, 57, 71, 84, 90; Chevening: 36/2; Clwyd Record Office: 107, 114, 120; Courtauld Institute: 36/2, 65, 67, 77, 79; Edinburgh University Library: 20; Granger Collection: 98; Harvard University Portrait Collection: 23; Illustrated London News Picture Library: 143, 200; Leger Galleries: 48; Mansell Collection: 33, 45, 46, 70, 96, 103, 119, 122, 124, 126, 127, 131, 134, 136, 146, 163, 165, 169, 170/1, 170/2, 172/1, 182, 184, 188-9, 194; Mary Evans Picture Library: 12, 37, 92, 110, 116; National Portrait Gallery: 27, 36/1, 43, 53, 197/1, 197/2; Radio Times Hulton Picture Library: 14, 15, 63, 72, 74, 86, 108, 112, 117, 151, 160, 172/2, 178, 179, 186, 190, 205; The Tate Gallery, London: 41; Victoria & Albert Museum: 59, 94; Weidenfeld & Nicolson Ltd: 73, 98, 166; YTV (Brian Cleasby): 50-1, 80-1, 104-5, 140-1, 154-5, 202-3.

Picture research by Deborah Pownall

Author's Note

The conversations and dialogue in this book are taken, on the whole, from my television plays, *Number 10*. They can be most fairly described as interpretations of the record; I do not claim them to be verbatim. The elements which blend in them are diaries, memoirs, letters, an assessment of the character, manner and personal style of the people concerned and a consideration of the events in which they were framed.

Introduction

'If walls of brick and stone can hold, for all time, some intangible deposit of the great events which once took place within their span, no human dwelling should have a richer heritage than Number 10 Downing Street. It is the "house of history" in which the past is a living presence not to be put by.'

Lady Violet Bonham Carter

Number 10 Downing Street, the world's most celebrated address, could also be called 'the house of crises', for not only has the destiny of Great Britain been shaped within its walls, but the families in residence have suffered the personal upheavals of political life as well as the common errings of human nature. Not all Prime Ministers have actually lived in Number 10, but those who have made it their home, some with their spouses and children, others with their mistresses, have also brought to the house their honour and venality, their friendships and enmities.

Described by an official who once served there as 'a gentleman's home in which a little government takes place from time to time', the house's unassuming narrow frontage reflects this characteristic English understatement. For, behind the simple entrance with its overhanging iron lamp surmounted by a crown, its black iron knocker in the shape of a lion's head, and the brass letter-box bearing the legend 'First Lord of the Treasury', there are sixty substantial rooms in which its famous and tempestuous tenants have wielded powers that have changed the course of Britain's political history and, often dramatically, that of their personal lives.

The present façade of the house dates back to 1772, though it lacks the beautiful proportions that are typical of the Georgian style. But, once through the open door, the visitor steps into a black and white marble tiled hall with a sunny, grey and gold wallpaper, which instantly hints at the spacious elegance beyond. Immediately to the left is a door leading to Number 11 Downing Street, the official residence of the Chancellor of the

11

Gladstone – fourth from the right – and his Cabinet meeting in the Cabinet Room at Number 10 in 1870

Exchequer. Next to this door, on a gilt, Kent-style table, is a book which every visitor must sign.

Most callers are first shown into a waiting-room graced with paintings loaned by the National Gallery. This was an arrangement initiated by Mr Ramsay MacDonald when he first took office in 1929, because he found the official portraits hanging in most rooms dull and unattractive.

Along a corridor leading to the Cabinet Room a tell-tale row of pegs labelled with impressive names reminds anyone who might think they were in a gentlemen's club that they are, in fact, on the threshold of the British Commonwealth's nerve centre. The Lord Chancellor, the Lord President of the Council, the Lord Privy Seal, the Chancellor of the Exchequer, and each member of the Cabinet has his own hook on which to hang his hat and coat.

The Cabinet Room itself is on ground floor level from Downing Street, but lies on the first floor overlooking the garden at the back, as the house is built on a slope. It is large, lofty, painted white, and lined with glass-fronted bookcases, some containing books presented by members of successive Cabinets, each signed by the donor – a practice started by Ramsay MacDonald. The room is dominated by two white Corinthian columns, and there is one picture – of Sir Robert Walpole.

Other than Cabinet members, no one may attend meetings unless specifically invited by the Prime Minister. To ensure total secrecy and security, all the windows and doors are doubled, only a Cabinet Minister may open or close the door, and every piece of paper used but not needed for official records is burnt in the grate.

Among the silver are a William III box, a pair of Queen Anne candlesticks, a pair of Georgian candlesticks donated by Lord Avon, and one owned by Pitt, and given by Lord Rosebery to Mr Harold Macmillan.

The Prime Minister has the only armchair of a red leather upholstered set, the other members of the Cabinet having to sit upright. A bell is close at hand to summon secretaries, as well as a telephone with a direct line to Her Majesty the Queen, wherever she may be in the world.

The Cabinet table was originally rectangular, but was replaced by a coffin-shape, designed by Mr Harold Macmillan. He liked to be able to see everyone's face from where he sat and the coffin-conformation was the geometric shape which served.

A wide flight of stairs leads from the entrance hall to the first floor. Its left-hand wall is lined with the portraits of every Prime Minister who has lived at Number 10 since 1721 – and it is the custom for each Prime Minister to donate his or her portrait on leaving office. On the landing, among other pictures, there is a Turner of an *Italian Landscape* and a small figure of Pitt. At the top of the stairs lies a small and comfortably furnished room overlooking Horse Guards' Parade, which has been used by many Prime Ministers as a study.

On the first floor are three drawing rooms: the white, the blue and the pillared. The white is in Adam style, the blue in Chippendale and the pillared was by William Kent. An intriguing detail of the pillared room is the multicoloured Tabriz carpet with a curious Persian inscription reading, 'I have no refuge in the world other than thy threshold. My head has no protection other than this porchway. The work of a slave of the Holy Place, Maqsud of Kashan in the year 926.' The walls of all three rooms are hung with portraits by Romney, Gainsborough and Reynolds.

Further along the landing lies the State Dining Room, leading first into a smaller dining room and then to the spacious State Drawing Room which is used for official receptions. No more than two hundred people are allowed here at a time owing to the age of the house and the frailty of the floors. At one time during his first term of office Ramsay MacDonald, enjoying a concert from the Orpheus Choir in a drawing room upstairs, found that their concentrated weight put them in grave danger of crashing through to the level below.

The official kitchen, occupying the south-east corner of the house, is the tallest room, rising through two storeys from the basement. It has a vaulted ceiling and a large semi-circular window facing east, an architectural feature clearly visible from the Whitehall end of Downing Street. It is dominated by a fourteen-foot-long table with a separate chopping block, which are both reputed to be more than two hundred years old and used for

The State Dining Room at Number 10, which was designed for William Pitt. This photograph shows the room at the beginning of this century

catering to William Pitt the Younger's lavish appetite for meat. It was here, too, that Lord North had meals prepared for twenty poor people every Sunday in the late 1770s.

On moving into the house, most Prime Ministers have brought their own furniture. They have never, however, been allowed to sell, give away or otherwise dispose of any that was already there which they did not like, and to make sure of this a complete inventory of the plate and furniture has always been made on a change of occupants.

The British Constitution has grown slowly, and it took two hundred years for the office of Prime Minister to be recognized by law. It was not until the Minister for the Crown Act was passed in 1937 that the head of the Government was actually paid as such. Even then he was called 'Prime Minister and First Lord of the Treasury', the latter title being the office held by the King's chief executive minister at the beginning of the eighteenth century.

*Robert Walpole, Britain's first Prime Minister. He moved into Number 10 Downing
Street on 22 September 1735*

When George I ascended the throne in 1714, Sir Robert Walpole soon became virtually his spokesman in Parliament, and Leader of the House on the Crown's behalf. This position at first depended entirely on the King approving of his political and, indeed, general behaviour.

As Walpole gradually assumed the role of middleman between the legislative and executive parts of the State, it became evident that the King's authority depended more and more on his First Minister's command over Parliament. When Walpole failed to hold this vital domination due to political intrigue, he resigned. This marked a turning point in British constitutional history, for it underlined the fact that though it was essential for the head of government to possess the confidence of the King, it was equally essential for him to have the confidence of the House.

In 1721 George I appointed Walpole First Lord of the Treasury and Chancellor of the Exchequer, and as such he took the reins of government more firmly in hand. As he became more powerful, so the suggestion that the King had more confidence in one man than in any other caused resentment and, in fact, the title of *Prime* Minister was first bandied about as a sneer – to which Walpole objected strongly: 'Having first invested me with a kind of mock dignity and styled me PRIME Minister, they impute to me an unpardonable abuse of the chimerical authority which they only have erected and conferred. I unequivocally deny that I am SOLE and PRIME Minister.'

Though William Pitt the Younger mentioned that it was essential to have a minister 'possessing the chief weight in the council and the Principal place in the confidence of the king', the attacks and protests went on for many years.

Gladstone said of the post, 'Nowhere is there a man who has so much power with so little to show for it.'

And this has always been true.

As far as Number 10 Downing Street is concerned, Prime Ministers have always had to pay all the running costs, the wages and salaries of domestic staff and all the expenses of entertaining. The Government pays for repairs to the building, for the wages and salaries of civil servants working for the office, but nothing else. In short, the only privilege a Prime Minister has ever enjoyed has been the one of living rent free at Number 10.

CHAPTER ONE

Downing and his Street

Downing Street was built by a spy. But one anticipates. . . . In the beginning was the road. Its name, unpretentiously, was The Street, sometimes known as Lekinstreet. It ran between Charing Cross and Westminster and is now known as Whitehall. Flanking it on either side were the kind of cottages and houses with front gardens tumbling with roses, sweet williams and columbines, that are now inhabited by bankers at weekends in sanctuaries like Lavenham, Constable's childhood home in Suffolk.

It is difficult to imagine the fusion of city squalor and country fair that was London in the early sixteenth century, when Henry VIII was on the throne. Certainly a bird's eye view of the City and Westminster would have been a great deal less crowded and confused than it is today. The Thames was certainly the same, flowing northwards to the east of Westminster; running parallel to the river was The Street.

Between The Street and the river stood York Place, the official London residence of the Archbishops of York, a palatial building with a chapel and a counting house, surrounded by smaller houses and fragrant expanses of greenery and gardens. Along the river front a continuous line of imposing mansions, the town houses of bishops and nobility, followed the north-eastern flow of the Thames to the City and St Paul's Cathedral. Across the roadway from York Place, to the west of The Street, there were humble cottages with small gardens and groups of dwellings separated by narrow lanes and alleys. There was a manor house called The Mote, which stood in sixty acres of pasture land and, further west, there were fields and woods and open countryside, of which only St James's Park, Green Park and Hyde Park now remain.

Several inns and shops lined The Street, which itself was little more than a lengthy field of churned mud cut into deep ruts by coaches and wagons.

Detail from Ralph Agas' map of London, 1579, showing Westminster Abbey, the Palace of Whitehall and the palaces along the Strand. The site of Downing Street lies just to the left of the lower of the two Tudor gatehouses on King Street

Most ladies and gentlemen, elaborately caped and ruffed, rode on horseback, enabling them to look down upon less fortunate pedestrians who tried to avoid breathing in the pungent smells from the open sewers.

The Street was dominated by the lifestyle of the Archbishop of York, Cardinal Wolsey, then residing in greater splendour than the King. Fat, heavy jowled, arrogant and ever dressed in red damasks and satins, he seldom made his way from York Place to the Court of Westminster without a huge procession preceded by men on horseback bearing huge silver crosses while he followed, humbly and hypocritically, seated on a mule.

Cardinal Wolsey, Archbishop of York, meekly seated upon a mule, with his entourage of retainers carrying silver crosses and maces, setting out from York Place to ride to the King's palace at Westminster. A pen and ink drawing from Cavendish's life of Wolsey

As Wolsey fell from power, so he began to give over to the King his princely residences of Hampton Court, Bridewell, The Mote, and York Place. When Henry VIII acquired York Place in 1529, he began to convert the Archbishop's residence into the Palace of Whitehall. He secured The Mote, the cottages, tenements, the inns and shops opposite, and had them all demolished to provide a site for his pleasures: tennis courts, bowling alleys, and a pheasant court were laid out; a pit for cockfighting was constructed next to a tiltyard for jousting and a bearpit for baiting. All this took place in an extensive area flanked to the north and west by open countryside, now Trafalgar Square and St James's Park, to the east by The Street, renamed Whitehall, and to the south by Westminster Abbey. Henry then had a new street built, named King Street, as access from his Palace to the recreational grounds.

An English cockpit in the early seventeenth century

A few years later, the King's cockfighting pit was converted into a theatre and some of the tennis courts and grounds were built on to provide housing for his courtiers. The Keeper of the Palace moved into one of these residences, known as Cockpit Lodgings. Through the reigns of Edward VI, Mary I and Elizabeth I, more buildings in the area were erected, destroyed by fire, put up again and added to, until, historical records indicate, a brewery known as the Axe, together with outhouses and gardens, occupied nearly the whole length of King Street, and Cockpit Lodgings became one house.

During Elizabeth I's reign, her Keeper of the Palace, Sir Thomas Knyvet, acquired leases on the Axe brewery and Le Pecocke Inn next door, and it is on the foundations of this group of buildings that the Prime Minister's residence now stands. The superstitious could claim that the address showed the first indications of becoming a 'house of crises' under Knyvet's occupation. On a November night, when James I was on the throne, the 5th to be precise of the year 1605, Sir Thomas as Justice of the Peace of Westminster was hauled out of bed and asked to search the House of Lords with armed attendants. In the vaults it was he who surprised Guy Fawkes busily laying down faggots and gunpowder underneath the Houses of Parliament.

Knyvet died in 1622 leaving his properties to his wife. She died a few months later and in turn left them to her niece Elizabeth Hampden, who converted the Axe brewery and Le Pecocke Inn into a residence for herself. This became known as Hampden House and stood next to the Cockpit Lodgings.

George Downing was born in 1623, towards the end of James I's reign. His father, Emmanuel Downing, and his uncle, John Winthrop (his mother's brother), came from wealthy East Anglian families and were fervent Puritans. When Charles I ascended the throne in 1625 they were among the first in the Puritan movement openly to resent the restrictions imposed on them by the new King's High Anglican clerics. In 1629, when George was six, his uncle drew up an agreement with others of his faith to emigrate to New England, finding his own country odious to live in. Being a man of law he made sure that the community he was taking with him would be self governing and would not, as other settlers before, come under the control of London.

Before leaving England John Winthrop was elected the first Governor of Massachusetts, and sailed to America from Southampton in 1630 with three ships, to be closely followed by another seven, in all carrying sixty horses, two hundred and forty cows and seven hundred passengers.

Emmanuel Downing did not go with his brother-in-law, though he had every intention of making the crossing within the year. But he was unaware that his wife, who had other ideas in mind, would use delaying tactics, pretending fear at the perilous journey and anxiety for the health and happiness of her children.

He eventually found out that the real problem was a simple desire for her son to be properly educated at a good university. In a letter to her brother she explained that she wanted George to stay in England 'till he hath either attayned to perfection in the arts hear, or that theer be sufficient means for to perfect him therein with you, wich I would be most glad to hear of: it would make me goe far nimbler to New Eng'.

As luck would have it the colony, now grown to over ten thousand, had decided it was time a college was established. With money and books bequeathed by one John Harvard, a university was founded in that man's name.

The Downings crossed the Atlantic in 1639, settled in Salem among ardent members of the Puritan Church and three years later, aged nineteen, George Downing was one of the first Harvard students to graduate, immediately getting himself appointed as a teacher to junior pupils at the university for a salary of £4 a year.

In England Civil War had now broken out, and this began to affect Massachusetts economically. The young George became restless and, discontented with his small income, found a job as a spiritual instructor to seamen, enabling him to sail for the West Indies. A letter from Barbados sent to a cousin at the time, gives insight into his character and his interest in money. 'I believe they have bought this year no less than a thousand Negroes and the more they bui the better able they are to buye, for in a yeare and a half they will earne, with God's blessing, as much as they cost.'

For a year he moved around the Caribbean, visiting the various islands, and whenever he wrote home he made it clear that his ambition was to become rich and that his energies were spent on finding opportunities to make money.

When the news came through that the Puritans in England had won a series of victories against the King, and that some settlers were going home from New England, he became impatient to return himself. He was poor, however, so day after day he walked the docks trying to find a captain who would take him aboard. Eventually he was offered the post of preacher by a devout shipowner.

His eloquent sermons during the voyage are said to have converted so many members of the crew that Downing realized his oratorical potential could hold the key to future fortune. On landing in England he therefore took over a derelict church and, with grandiose bible thumping, filled it to overflowing with open-mouthed congregations while other churches remained empty.

On the night of Charles I's execution he apparently became so impassioned while thanking God for the successful beheading, that even the most fanatical of his devotees were shocked into silence.

For a while he managed to earn a living by preaching and he started touring the country delivering sermons. In the North he secured an appointment with General Fairfax's army as preacher to Colonel Okey's regiment, and lost no time making use of new connections in high places. Soon, presumably using his well-practised powers of speaking, he was commissioned as Chief of the Intelligence Staff under Sir Arthur Haselrig, Governor of Newcastle.

In the summer of 1648, when the Civil War was nearly over and King Charles was a prisoner in the Isle of Wight, there was a fresh Royalist

A seventeenth-century portrait, presumed to be of Sir George Downing, from the Fogg Art Museum, Harvard University. A copy of this painting hangs in Downing College, Cambridge

uprising in the North and Oliver Cromwell travelled to Newcastle to suppress it. Downing made sure he would meet him and a year later, having
obviously made a good impression, he was appointed Chief of Intelligence
Staff to Cromwell's forces, bearing the title Scoutmaster General.

He was now twenty-six. His duties were to organize and control the spy
service, and for these he received an annual salary of £365 a year plus £4 a
day allowance to pay agents. He was undoubtedly good at his job, for one of
the reasons that Cromwell and Fairfax were so successful was the efficiency
of their intelligence.

There are no records of what George Downing actually did, which is not
surprising as he would have had all communications regarding his spy
work destroyed, but it is known from family letters that he increased his
income considerably from rents on properties he purchased, perhaps with
monies acquired from threatened enemies or persons about whom he knew
more than should be broadcast for their own comfort.

His position naturally brought him in close personal contact with the
highest authorities in the land and, after serving his country during the war
against the Dutch in 1652, he married the young, beautiful and rich sister
of the Earl of Carlisle in 1654. Shortly after this he was elected Member of
Parliament for Edinburgh, sitting in the first House of Commons of the
Protectorate.

In 1655 Cromwell sent him to France as an envoy to protest to Louis XIV
about the massacre of Protestants by the Duke of Savoy's troops. As was his
habit, Downing lost no opportunity and managed to arrange a meeting for
himself with Cardinal Mazarin, then the most powerful man in Europe. So
clever was he at infiltrating himself into the company of notable persons
that he wrote proudly to John Thurloe, then Secretary of State, 'Mazarin
sent me his owne supper with this complement, that it being too late to
provide anything, he had sent what was made ready for himselfe, and
would seek a supper himselfe; he also send me his owne plate and servants
to wayte, and the Captain of his guard.'

Throughout his life it was one of Downing's preoccupations to acquire as
many posts as possible. One such lucrative position was as a Teller at the
Exchequer, with rooms in Whitehall and a clerk assigned to him named
Samuel Pepys. The diarist wrote of his new employer, 'So stingy a fellow is
he, I care not to see him!'

However stingy he may have been, Downing apparently knew whose
palm to grease, for Cromwell now appointed him Ambassador to the Hague
with a salary of £1,000 per annum. At the age of thirty-two he had married
well, been elected a Member of Parliament, and was honoured by this new
post. Downing now set about acquiring interests in land west of Whitehall
which, in time, would unwittingly guarantee him his place in history.

In the late 1650s the Dutch were not only Britain's greatest trading rivals, but also more powerful at sea. They were, however, Protestants and Cromwell's main interest was to further the Protestant cause against the Alliance formed by the Pope, the Holy Roman Empire and the exiled claimant to the throne, Charles II.

Downing's post as Ambassador was, in fact, a cover. For, living in The Hague was Charles II's sister, Mary, married to William, Prince of Orange, who was constantly planning the Stuart restoration.

Downing was again a spy.

With a great deal of experience at his finger tips he quickly set up a network of agents in Holland and all over the Continent which enabled him to gain extraordinary power. Whenever he learned that Charles or his brothers, the Dukes of York and Gloucester, were planning a visit to their sister, Downing was able to block them by protesting secretly to the Dutch Council of State who stopped them coming into the country. By the same means he also managed to forbid English ministers living in Holland, who had Royalist tendencies, praying for their future King, which did not make him any more popular.

In a letter to a friend in England, a certain John Lane in The Hague wrote of Downing at the time:

He is a fearful gentleman. The day after the Princess came to town he set two of his footmen to stand sentry the whole day, one on the top of the stairs before the door, the other at the corner of the house, to watch the back gate, but there has been none since. He has hired another house. I hope the next remove of him and the rest of his comrades will be to the gallows, where they may have their due reward.

Using blackmail Downing secured the services of Charles's trusted courtiers – in one instance, those of Tom Howard, the Earl of Suffolk's brother, about whom he reported to Thurloe, 'He had a whoor in this country, with which he trusted his secrets and papers: these two afterwards falling out, a person in this town got all the papers from her.'

Aware that if his skulduggery came to light he might well be assassinated, he wrote further to Thurloe, 'If it should be known that I have given you this account he would endeavour to have me killed.'

No doubt, despite his heartless streak combined with a first-class brain, he was occasionally frightened, especially for his wife and children who were at The Hague with him.

It was part of Downing's established system to have every paper, letter and document that he received copied and sent to Thurloe. But when Cromwell died in 1658 he became more cautious. Uncertain whether the Protectorate would survive or whether the King would be successfully brought back by the Royalists, he sent only some of the information which came into his possession.

Cromwell had named his son as successor, but trouble was brewing and

Charles II, still a king in exile, dancing with his sister Mary at the court in The Hague. A painting by Janssens

by 1659 Richard Cromwell had been forced to abdicate. Downing shrewdly started to play a double game. When news came to him that Charles was making an attempt to visit his sister in The Hague, he made no protestations but on the contrary paid the King a visit, disguised as an old man. Revealing his identity, he advised His Majesty to leave the country at once before the Dutch authorities could arrest him and hand him over to his enemies in England. Times were uncertain.

General Monck, who had served Charles I but later changed his loyalties to Cromwell, was a key figure, though remaining for the time being in the background. Following skirmishes between rival forces in London, Monck marched his army down from Coldstream* in Scotland to the capital, implying that he was on the side of the Commonwealth. A day later, however, he made contact secretly with the exiled Charles.

Learning of this, Downing acted swiftly and let it be known that he was swearing allegiance to the Crown. If the King could forgive him his Puritan past and accept his services, he was ready to work on the major forces in the army, among whom he wielded considerable influence.

* When Charles II was restored to the throne, Monck's regiment became known as the Coldstream Guards, one of the King's household guards regiments, in recognition of the part they played in the re-establishment of the monarchy in England.

George Monck, 1st Duke of Albemarle, the founder of the Coldstream Guards. As General Monck, he was a key figure in Charles II's restoration, and was given as a reward for his services a dukedom and the Cockpit Lodgings for his London home

Downing was so careful during this time that, again, he left no traces of what he actually did. But he must have served the King well for, before sailing for England, Charles II knighted him in Holland on 21 May 1660. Pepys records in his diaries that Downing 'called me to him to tell me that I must write him SIR G. Downing!'.

On his return to London with his wife and family, a few days after the King, Downing learned that the properties he had acquired to the west of Whitehall had been taken back by the Crown. The land was originally Crown property and as the sale had been made by Cromwell's Parliamentary Commission, without royal consent, it was declared null and void at the Restoration.

Downing was determined to get back his properties, but though he had made his peace with the Royalists he was not too sure what the King really thought of him. Wisely he chose to keep his head down and for a time moved quietly about the offices of Whitehall, visiting new ministers and advising the newly formed Council of Trade; his skill at negotiating trade agreements with Holland was appreciated.

Eventually the King reappointed him Ambassador to The Hague. It was an opportunity to prove himself anew, and he did so with zealous enthusiasm. The King was determined to punish all those who had been responsible for his father's execution. Some of the regicides had been arrested in England, but many others had managed to escape to the Continent. Downing realized that one way of gaining favour was by rounding them up, even if it meant searching the whole of Europe.

While negotiating the treaty of alliance, he therefore persuaded the Dutch government to insert a clause whereby any regicides living in the country would be surrendered. He then offered his agents a prize of £200 for every enemy of the King inveigled on to Dutch soil and arrested.

Several such people were instantly located in Europe, among them Downing's first commander, Colonel Okey, in whose regiment he had been so thankful to serve as preacher. Being a kind and grateful soul, Downing immediately wrote to Okey and assured him that he would be safe in Holland, knowing the man was interested in visiting The Hague on business. He then obtained a warrant for his arrest from the Dutch authorities, and waited.

The moment Okey arrived, Downing paid him a visit with a few of his footmen, about which he wrote:

Knocking at ye doore one of ye house came to see who it was and ye doore being open, the under Scout and ye whole company rushed immediately into ye house, and into ye roome where they were sitting by a fyere side with pipe of tobacco and a cup of beere, immediately they started up to have gott out at a back doore but it was too late, ye roome was in a moment fulle. They made many excuses, ye one to have got liberty to have fetch his coate and another to goe to privy all in vayne.

This action did not endear Downing to his contemporaries and a pamphlet of the time broadcast:

This Generous and Plainhearted Colonel did without the least hesitation respose a great deal of Trust and confidence in one whom he had been instrumental to raise from the dust; little thinking that his New England Tottered Chaplain whom he Cloathed and Fed at his table, and who dipped with him in his own dish, should prove like the Devil among the twelve to his Lord and Master.

After a brief period in the Tower, Okey and his friends were sentenced to death on 16 April 1662 and executed at Tyburn three days later.

Pepys wrote of this incident, 'G. Downing (like a perfidious rogue) though the action is good and of service to the King, yet he cannot with any good conscience do it. All the world takes notice of him for a most ungrateful villain for his pains.'

John Evelyn dismissed Downing in his diaries as 'a pedagogue and fanatic preacher not worth a grote who insinuated himself into the King's favour and became excessive rich'.

But Charles II was grateful and Downing received a baronetcy and a letter of congratulations from the Government. 'We doe heere al magnify your diligente and prudente conduct in the seisinge and conveyinge over of the regicides and we thinke few others would have used such dexterity, or would have compassed so difficult a business.'

It was a good moment to bring up the question of the Whitehall land. Downing wrote to the King claiming that the property had come to him as a debt, and that he had been forced to accept it because the money was owed to him, a statement unsupported by any evidence. The King, however, granted his plea and on 23 February 1664 he was given the lease of the site and buildings standing on it:

All that messuage or house in Westminster, with all the courts, gardens and orchards thereto, situate between a certain house or mansion called the Peacock in part and the common sewer in part on the South side and a gate leading to King Street called the New Gate in part, and an old passage leading to a court called Pheasant Court in part, and an old passage leading from the great garden to St James's Park in part, on the North side, and abutting on King Street on the East side and upon the wall of St James's Park on the West side.

Downing was further given permission to build, subject to the supervision of the Surveyor-General of Crown Lands, and with the proviso that construction would go no further than the west part of the house called the Cockpit, which meant no closer to the park than where Number 10 now stands.

Having obtained building permission, he now intended to pull down Hampden House and use the entire area to erect a row of houses running

A detail from Elizabeth Foster's 'Accurate plan of the cities of London and Westminster', 1752, showing Westminster, Whitehall and St James's Park. Downing Street can be seen to the left of the Privy Garden of Whitehall

east to west from Whitehall to the park. But Elizabeth Hampden's grand-sons, her heirs, put up a fight, not wanting to surrender what remained of their lease which still had twenty years to run. So Downing's endeavours to get possession failed, despite his complaints that 'The houseing are in great decay and will hardly continue to be habitable to the end.'

He had to wait.

In 1665 Downing was appointed Secretary to the Treasury and lived in Stephens Court, opposite the House of Commons. By divine right of kingly contrariness, Charles II had discovered that he did not like Downing too much and decided to send him back to The Hague. He was warned that there might be danger for Downing there because of his unpopularity. It is reported that on hearing this His Majesty smiled wryly and said, 'I will venture him!'

The predictions proved correct, and after three months in Holland, Downing fled back to London, fearing the mounting indignation of the Dutch both at his past and his presence. The King promptly had him arrested for deserting his post and he was sent to the Tower for six weeks, thus tasting a spoonful of his own medicine. He was never to regain favour completely.

Alterations to Cockpit Lodgings behind Hampden House were now in progress on behalf of the King's friend, the Duke of Buckingham, who had been brought up with Charles I's children and on the outbreak of the Civil War had accompanied the Prince of Wales to Scotland, and thence escaped into exile.

This large house had had its share of nobility, for in 1606 Sir Thomas Knyvet had vacated it so that Charles I, then only a four-year-old prince, could live there. His sister, Princess Elizabeth, moved in when she was eight, and to accommodate her household a kitchen and living quarters for domestic staff had been added. After she married the Elector Palatine in 1613 the house reverted to the use of the Keeper of the Palace, first Lord Rochester, then the Earl of Pembroke, who stayed there until 1650, a year after Charles I's execution.

Oliver Cromwell himself then moved in and was resident for four years, leaving in 1654 to go across the road to the main Palace of Whitehall. In 1660, when Charles II returned to the throne, General Monck, now Duke of Albemarle, was given the house as well as some of the adjoining houses and two large gardens as his London home. He lived there during the desperate months of the Great Plague while others fled to the country.

Albemarle died in 1670 and Buckingham took over. When he fell out of favour, the house underwent further alterations for Lady Charlotte Fitzroy – the King's illegitimate daughter by Barbara Villiers, Duchess of Cleveland – who married the Earl of Lichfield. A whole storey was added so that the house now had five floors including basement and attic, and an enlarged garden looking out onto St James's Park where, under an abundance of trees, deer grazed among flowering shrubs.

Sir George Downing was now forty-eight and very aware that he had as many enemies among the Republicans as among the Royalists. To ensure himself an independent income, should he lose his contacts with Whitehall altogether, he was more determined than ever to build a new street of houses which he could rent.

With the Hampden House lease at last reverting to him, he applied for permission to build beyond the limit imposed earlier. When this was granted, he was able to start on his row of houses. Fifteen were erected with remarkable speed for the time. The largest house stretched right back towards the Countess of Lichfield's home, disturbing her so much that she wrote to the King, her father, protesting at the loss of privacy. The King replied:

> I think it a very reasonable thing that other houses should not look into your house without your permission, and this note will be sufficient for Mr Surveyor to build up your wall as high as you please, the only caution I give you is not to prejudice the corner house, which you know your sister Sussex is to have, and the building up the wall there will signify nothing to you, only inconvenience her.

The corner house in which 'sister Sussex' was to live stood on the site that now holds Number 12 Downing Street. Sussex was Anne, the King's elder daughter by Barbara Villiers.

When Downing's street of houses was finally completed, Charles II gave permission for it to be named Downing Street, but Sir George, that 'perfidious rogue and doubly perjured traitor' as Pepys called him, was never to live there. Among other properties that he had acquired all over the country was an estate in Cambridge where he had settled his ageing mother and which was to become his home. He retired there in 1675 to die, aged sixty-one, in July 1684.

The Lichfields left the house in Cockpit Lodgings in the late 1680s and the next occupant was Mr d'Auverquerque, one of William III's Dutch courtiers and Master of the Horse. On becoming naturalized and receiving an English peerage, he changed his name to Lord Overkirk. He and his wife lived there for eighteen years till his death in 1708.

Lady Overkirk stayed on for a further twelve years, after which the house again became Crown property and was extensively renovated for Baron von Bothmar, the German nobleman who had come to England ten years previously as the accredited representative of the Elector of Hanover, heir presumptive to the English throne.

Because all of Queen Anne's children had died, Bothmar was regarded by

Downing Street in 1827, from a watercolour by J. C. Buckley. Number 10 is the second door on the right

many as the virtual ruler of England during the last years of her reign. He did not like the house, which was a constant source of irritation to him, and complained about it continually. He died in 1732 and it was then that the Prime Minister, Sir Robert Walpole, took it over. Walpole thought it too small for his needs, so acquired the Crown lease on the adjacent Downing Street house and commissioned William Kent, the Palladian architect, to join the two together.

The premises were completely redesigned, a new staircase was put in, the larger house's entrance from the park was closed, and a new one into Downing Street opened. The alterations took three years to complete and on 22 September 1735, Number 10 was finally occupied by its first Prime Minister.

The house had been offered to him by the Crown as a gift. But, old fox that he was, Walpole knew the foundations were built on the shifting silt that came up from the Thames and that the structure would be a constant source of expense. He therefore humbly declared himself unworthy of the gift, but accepted it on behalf of all future First Lords of the Treasury in perpetuity.

From now on, the State paid the builder's men.

CHAPTER TWO

Bloodline

William Pitt the Younger was born in 1759 during the Seven Years War: George II was on the English throne, Louis XV was King of France; and General Wolfe was killed attacking Quebec, having been sent to Canada to expel the French by William's father, Pitt the Elder, then Secretary of State. 1759 was to be regarded later as the 'Year of Victories', with not only Quebec gained for the British but battles won at Minden, Lagos and Quiberon Bay. In India, Robert Clive was driving out the French and history would record that 1759 was also to be the year of the birth of the British Empire.

The Pitts were a well-established family descended from rich landowners and a seventeenth-century Commissioner of the Navy. William's great-grandfather was Governor of Madras, an extremely capable man with few scruples. He became known as 'Diamond' Pitt, having purchased an exceptionally large diamond in India, which he later sold for a handsome profit to the Regent of France.

'Diamond' Pitt had several sons, one of whom went into Parliament, starting a family tradition, for in time his sons followed in his footsteps and his nephew, Pitt the Elder, joined the powerful family political party within the House of Commons.

The Pitts married well, and became connected with such illustrious families as the Lytteltons, the Cholmondeleys, the Fauconburgs and the Londonderrys. Though 'Diamond' Pitt died an extremely rich man, his fortune was so shared out among these families, who all knew only too well how to spend it, that little was left for the next generation. Pitt the Elder therefore had the background of wealth, but not the income to go with it.

In Parliament Pitt the Elder was in opposition to Sir Robert Walpole's Government and was disliked by the King, but his power in the House of Commons could not be denied. While Walpole tried to keep the peace, Pitt

William Pitt the Elder, 1st Earl of Chatham, from a portrait painted in about 1754 by Hoare

Lady Hester Grenville, painted by Hudson. William Pitt the Younger inherited his distinct profile from his mother

the Elder was all for declaring war against Spain in order to protect British trade, only intending to fight the enemy in South America and on the High Seas. But the conflict escalated and soon Europe became involved.

In 1744 he suffered the first of three mental breakdowns which were to threaten his political career. He survived, temporarily, returned to the House and guided himself towards the highest offices in the land, but the King loathed him so much that he was again forced to retire.

In 1754, aged forty-five, he married Lady Hester Grenville, the thirty-three-year-old daughter of Lord Cobham of Stowe. She devotedly nursed him through another illness and managed his finances, presenting him the next year with their first child, Hester, followed by John in 1756, Harriot in 1758, William in 1759 and James Charles two years later.

William's early childhood was spent in Hayes Place in Kent, a twenty-four bedroomed house surrounded by elegant gardens standing in several hundred acres of pasture and woodland. His father inherited a second mansion at Burton Pynsent in Somerset, so that the family divided their time between the two.

Pitt the Elder became Prime Minister in 1766. So great was his prestige that wherever the children went they were regarded with awe by the majority of people they met. When the family went on holiday to the coast, villagers would strew flowers in front of their carriage as they passed.

The children were educated at home by a private tutor from Cambridge University. At seven William was by far the brightest of all the children in the family, indeed he was brighter than most children of his age. Whereas

Hayes Place in Kent, the childhood home of William Pitt

'The Bottomless Pitt', a caricature attributed to Gilray showing Pitt as Chancellor of the Exchequer at the dispatch box in the House of Commons, introducing his budget in 1792

John, destined to inherit the new earldom of Chatham bestowed on his father, was earmarked for the Army and James for the Navy, it was taken for granted that William would go into politics.

He was a delicate little boy and often ill. The family doctor surprisingly diagnosed early signs of gout, which he thought might be inherited, and for this often painful illness he prescribed a number of nasty medicaments which the poor boy took without a murmur.

As soon as he could read and write, William was as much at home in Latin and French as he was in English. By the time he was eleven he would write in the most precocious way, usually to his father, in the following vein, 'I flatter myself that the sun shone on your expedition and that the views were enough enlivened thereby to prevent the drowsy Morpheus from taking the opportunity of the heat to diffuse his poppies upon the eyes of the traveller.' Which, conveyed in simpler terms, meant he hoped that his father had had a pleasant sunny journey.

His father had considered William too delicate for public school, but, so that he should not be unaware of the barbarities of the system, he one day had him comprehensively flogged in the garden by young Hiley Addington, his doctor's son.

It was in the garden, too, that Chatham laid the foundations of his son's phenomenal debating and oratorical talents. He would put little William on a tree stump, point to a stand of trees and say: 'There is the Opposition. The subject is such-and-such. Speak.'

It was this training, plus careful education in all the niceties of parliamentary behaviour, that made the young Pitt, on entering the Commons at twenty-two, feel not at all alien, but 'as if he had come home'. His maiden speech signalled the future. Maiden speeches are usually diligently prepared, but William had no such chance. On his entering the Chamber in the middle of a debate, he was recognized and a chant went up, 'Pitt, Pitt, Pitt'. He thereupon picked up a point from the previous speaker's argument, demolished it in a paragraph and went on with a forty-five minute disquisition of his own, so scintillating that Edmund Burke remarked openly, ''Tis not a chip off the old block. 'Tis the old block himself.'

The person least surprised by this would have been his home tutor. In 1773, when William was fourteen, he was sent to Pembroke Hall at Cambridge, his tutor's own college, so that his course of education would not be interrupted. Concerning the decision to send him there, his tutor wrote,

I could not have acted with more prudence than I have done in the affair of Pembroke Hall. Mr Pitt is not the child his years bespeak him to be. He has now all the understanding of a man. He has sound principles, a grateful and liberal heart, and talents unequalled. He will go to Pembroke, not a weak boy to be made a property of, but to be admired as a prodigy; not to hear lectures but to spread light. His parts are most astonishing and universal. He will be perfectly qualified for a wrangler before he goes, and will be an accomplished classick, mathematician, historian and poet. This is no exaggeration.

Shortly after taking up residence in the college, young Pitt fell ill again and had to return to Somerset. His doctor, quite certain now that the boy was suffering from gout, prescribed the treatment of one bottle of port wine a day, which helped him recover, even though it was to cause him an addiction to the wine for the rest of his life.

At seventeen William, studying law, started to enjoy the university's social life. Although never too gregarious, he was sought after for company as he was reported to be 'abounding in playful wit and quick repartee' and described as 'by far the most agreeable and popular man among the undergraduates'.

When he could he visited Westminster to listen to his father in Opposition in the House of Lords, and was quite critical about the effect the various speeches had on their Lordships. Pitt the Elder, now the Earl of Chatham, enjoyed a powerful use of the language and such a brilliant delivery that even David Garrick, the adulated actor, was said to be jealous.

In 1778 the Earl of Chatham collapsed in the House while making a speech against American Independence. He was taken to Hayes Place where he died a few weeks later. He had suffered bouts of mental illness throughout his life which was inherent in other members of the family, for when William's younger sister Anne came to London from a tour of Europe for the funeral, she had to be confined to a home shortly afterwards. She died there two years later.

The family now looked to William to get them through the aftermath of the Earl's death. John, in the Army, was with his regiment in Gibraltar and it fell to William to settle his father's affairs. Though too young to inherit anything himself, he knew that when he came of age he would receive a legacy of £3,500 – a tidy sum in the eighteenth century. He therefore borrowed from relatives and friends and, having been admitted to Lincoln's Inn, moved into rooms there. Within a few months, extravagant by nature, he found London so expensive that he was obliged to mortgage the rooms in order to live, an indication of the way he would manage his money for the rest of his life. Early on he had learned to enjoy luxurious surroundings and the extravagant ways that went with them, but he was capable of totally ignoring how it could all be paid for. If it could be so called, he had the gift of complete financial indifference.

William Pitt was called to the bar in 1780. At twenty-one he decided to follow seriously in his father's footsteps and stood as member of Parliament for Cambridge University, but failed to be elected. But the following year he was returned as member for Appleby in Westmorland, and on 23 January

John Singleton Copley's dramatic reconstruction of the scene in the House of Lords on 7 July 1778 when Chatham collapsed while making an emotional speech against granting the Americans independence. He was to die at Hayes Place a few weeks later

1781 he took his seat in the House of Commons. There he joined his father's followers, the Chathamites under Lord Shelburne, in opposition to Lord North's administration.

In 1782 Lord Rockingham succeeded North and offered William the post of Vice-Treasurer to Ireland, which carried a salary of £5,000 per annum. Despite the fact that he could well do with such an income, young Pitt refused the position, not wanting a subordinate post. At twenty-three he had definite ideas about his career, an attitude which was much respected. When Rockingham died in July of the same year, Shelburne became Prime Minister and appointed William Chancellor of the Exchequer and Leader of the House. As such he moved into Number 10 in August, Shelburne having no desire to move from his own residence in Berkeley Square.

As far as Pitt was concerned, it was 'The best Summer Town House possible', though vast and awkward. He immediately spent £700 on alterations, which could have been a waste of time and money for shortly after, Charles James Fox, who was to become his political rival for life, formed a coalition with Lord North and forced Shelburne out of office.

George III wanted Pitt to form a government. The young parliamentarian had displayed incredible talents in the House and it was an amazing offer, but it was not made to a fool and Pitt saw clearly that the time for him to take the premier office was not right. His refusal meant that he had to move out of Number 10, and a coalition ministry was formed under the Duke of Portland, with Charles James Fox and Lord North as joint Secretaries of State. But this ministry collapsed after only ten months and George III returned to the young Pitt. This time he accepted the offer and became Britain's youngest Prime Minister, returning to Downing Street at the age of twenty-four.

When his appointment was announced, it was greeted in the House by a good deal of jeering, laughter and doubt. It was unlikely that one so young could speak in all the major debates in the face of hostile opposition, and of ambitious enemies who would now become maliciously devious.

But Pitt was not one to get involved with in-fighting or even party politics. He was resolute in his ideas and ideals and simply got on with the business of governing. He was against a quarrel with America, he was bent on parliamentary reform, he wanted a union with Ireland and Catholic emancipation, he hoped to reorganize the East India Company, and he intended to reduce the National Debt.

During his first year in office he suffered many defeats and setbacks, but he soldiered on unperturbed and, when he thought the moment was right, he dissolved Parliament in 1784 to go to the country. In March he won overwhelmingly in the election, was returned as Tory Prime Minister and became one of the most powerful ministers of English history.

He succeeded in reducing the National Debt, introduced a sinking fund, and passed the India Act establishing a Board of Control over all the British territorial possessions in the East Indies and over the affairs of the East India Company. But in the following year things were less easy and both his Reform Bill and Union of Ireland Bill were rejected, and in 1788 he had to fight agitation regarding the slave trade. To add to his mounting problems, George III became mentally ill. Pitt had had enough experience of what an unstable mind was like in his own family, and he managed to cope with the monarch. But again Fox in Opposition caused him unnecessary problems, insisting that a Regency under the Prince of Wales should take over the power of the throne. He weathered these storms and by 1789 the King had recovered. But if Pitt had hopes of sitting back a little, he saw a black cloud loom across the Channel.

The French Revolution broke out in July. Slowly but surely everything that had upheld the French *ancien régime* started to crumble, causing waves of fear among the richer families in England. With the rise of Napoleon Bonaparte, war with France became inevitable. Pitt, now twenty-eight, had the country behind him and a reliable government; all he needed was

The House of Commons in 1793, from a painting by Hickel. William Pitt is shown to the left of the dispatch box, with his feet carefully placed behind the line so that he is not ruled out of order according to parliamentary rules. His great rival, the saturnine Charles James Fox, is depicted with hat and stick, to the right of the Speaker's chair

to have a clear head to steer the ship through the inevitable whirlpool of conflict.

But William, though extremely shy, was not all work and no play; he was aware that he needed to relax on occasions, and in order to do so he rented a house on Putney Heath to which he escaped whenever he could. The house in Somerset where his mother lived was too far to go for short stays, and it is clear that he regretted not having her closer to share his political successes. He wrote to her once, 'I only wish you were a nearer spectator and that I could have the opportunity of telling you all you would like to hear.' He was also concerned that she was not well off, and though his own finances were as always unstable, he tried to reassure her that she need have no worries. 'The income of the Lord of the Treasury and Chancellor of the Exchequer together will really furnish more than my expenses can require; and I hope I need not say the surplus will give me more satisfaction than all the rest, if it can contribute to diminish embarrassment where least of all any ought, I am sure, to subsist.'

The one woman who provided the necessary female element in his social life was Harriot his sister, older by one year, who had not yet married. Charming, witty and vivacious, she moved into Number 10 in 1785 to act as his hostess. It was generally said of her that it was a pity she was his sister, for no other woman in the world was so suited to be his wife.

William Pitt was to make Number 10 more his home than any other Prime Minister after him, for he was to live there for nineteen years. In the 1780s Downing Street was a cul-de-sac with houses across the west end: Number 10 was the only residence with government connections, so Pitt had private neighbours. The house was larger than it looked, having recently been extended by North and Rockingham at a cost of £10,000, a vast sum considering that for the seven preceding years only £500 a year had been spent on it. The alterations had consisted of a new and extremely convenient kitchen, offices and several comfortable lodging rooms, but most of the money had been spent on consolidating the foundations.

A stable and coach house stood across the open ground to the east of the house, while to the north, a study and dining room overlooked the agreeable garden. The dining room was furnished with nineteen mahogany chairs around a large mahogany table. Pitt's prized collection of books, dating back from his Cambridge days – classics, history, mathematics – lined the walls of the library which lay between his secretary's office and his study.

Though he was not in a position to do so, Pitt now decided to purchase a country house of his own and bought a small mansion, Holwood House in Kent, on a mortgage he could not afford. As far as he was concerned, Holwood was a most beautiful spot, but its purchase a foolish extravagance.

Indifferent to money, he spent about twice his income on his comfort, which included the comfort of his stomach, for he never saved on anything. He also encouraged others to live well. Harriot wanted to marry the son of Lord Eliot, but the latter was reluctant to approve the match because Edward Eliot was not well off. Pitt learned that the young man was due to inherit a small fortune on coming of age, so he persuaded the father to see things differently. 'A further delay, such as you now desire, could not I am persuaded be reconciled to the happiness of either of them, or under all the circumstances be productive of any possible advantage.' A provisional settlement was made payable once Edward had come into his inheritance, and Harriot was happily married in September. The couple spent most of their time at Number 10, where Harriot continued to act as her brother's hostess.

At about this time Pitt suffered a minor setback in his health. A cyst on the face, which had troubled him earlier in his Cambridge days, flared up and promised to be dangerous unless it was removed. A room in Downing

Holwood House in Kent, the country home of William Pitt

Street was turned into a surgery and the Prime Minister stoically bore the intense pain of various incisions without an anaesthetic, not even having his hands tied down, as was the practice. He wrote about the unpleasant event to a friend, 'Having yesterday parted with the ornament on my cheek, and two or three handkerchiefs for the present occupying the place of it, my appearance is better suited to correspondence than conversation.'

Harriot became pregnant and was expecting her child the following September. It was decided that the baby should be born at Number 10 and on the 20th of that month Pitt wrote to his mother, 'I have infinite joy in being able to tell you that my sister has just made me a present of a girl and that both she and our new guest are in every way as well as possible.' It was the first child to be born in the house since it had become the official residence of the First Lord of the Treasury, but unfortunately the event proved tragic, for two days later Harriot became seriously ill and died.

William Pitt was so shattered that he retired and would see no one for days afterwards. Parliamentary business was continued through his secretary and if his closest friends and colleagues were concerned about him, he was even more concerned for the sanity of his brother-in-law, Edward Eliot. Again he wrote to his mother, 'I will not suffer myself at this moment, my Dear Mother, to express my own feelings, which I know are too deeply yours

Jane, Duchess of Gordon, with whom William Pitt was linked romantically by many people. In her unconventional youth she rode down an Edinburgh street bareback on a pig

also. I should not lose a moment, you will believe, in coming to Somerset, but I am sure you will approve of my not leaving poor Eliot at this time.'

Edward remained at Number 10 and both men lived there quietly, not wanting to see anyone till they could recover from their painful, mutual loss.

The only other woman with whom William Pitt's name had been linked was Jane, Duchess of Gordon, the wife of Alexander, 4th Duke of Gordon, one of the richest men in England. She was an unconventional lady, witty, intelligent and attractive with a turn of phrase which was perhaps not entirely suitable for the best dinner tables. Her idea of a good time was singularly boisterous. Being so fond of animals and any sport connected with them, she once rode a pig bareback down an Edinburgh street, and was forever urging her male friends to indulge in similar escapades.

She was ten years older than Pitt, yet once she had parted from her husband, rumour had it that they might marry. Politically she was influential, surrounding herself with many of the younger parliamentarians, but her wish was not to wed the Prime Minister herself, but for her daughter Charlotte to do so. Charlotte, however, married the Duke of Richmond, and when Harriot died all three of them became Pitt's closest friends. The Duchess took over as his hostess at Number 10, which she called 'Bachelor Hall', for William was so fast becoming over-reserved and too shy to mix in society at all, that he was said to be living like a monk and with women he was like a statue.

With Napoleon active in France, he became totally obsessed with the defence of England. All those close to him gave up the idea of ever again seeing him as a normal happy-go-lucky individual until, unexpectedly, a young lady came onto the scene with an unprecedented effect on his life. Pitt had known her when she was a baby, and had more recently seen her when he had visited her parents at their home close to Holwood House*. Her name was Eleanor Eden, she was the daughter of Lord and Lady Auckland, who had been friends of the Pitt family for years, and when they came to visit him at Number 10 one afternoon, they brought her with them.

Polite and reserved on greeting his old friends, Pitt asked where little Eleanor was, to be surprised to learn from her mother that she was 'primping and smoothing herself in your pier glass in the hall'.

'Primping! Mudlark Eleanor? I've scarce ever seen her without earth on her face or blackberry juice on her cheeks!' the Prime Minister exclaimed.

When she entered the library he was astonished to see a twenty-year-old girl, dewy as a rose and stunningly beautiful. Taken aback he greeted her reservedly as 'Little Eleanor' to which she curtly replied, but with her eyes

---

* The Edens lived at Beckenham in Kent, close to Hayes and to Holwood. William Eden had also lived at Number 14 Downing Street and had been in Lord North's Cabinet.

Eleanor Eden, from a portrait by John Hoppner

sparkling, 'Hardly so diminutive, I would have said sir, I am, after all, twenty years old.'

He apologized, excusing his lapse on the grounds that when they had last met she was barely fourteen, which she promptly corrected to 'fourteen and seven months', which should have been an indication that she remembered a good deal more about their previous encounters than he did. 'We sat together against a hay wain and you explained to me how to solve the Irish Question,' she went on, then was reprimanded by her mother for being forward with, after all, a man who was Prime Minister of England.

Shortly after this first visit Pitt saw Eleanor Eden again. She accompanied him on several social occasions, and he even invited her back to Number 10, always, as was the custom for ladies, in the company of her maid.

He was now nearly forty, she twenty years younger, and it never occurred to him that other people might see the relationship as anything but innocent. But the Duchess of Gordon knew Young William and she was of the opinion that there was a streak of something in that icy demeanour of which nobody dreamed, and that sooner or later it would make itself obvious.

Eleanor was in fact far more mature for her age than William Pitt and it was clear that in her mind she had decided that the Prime Minister needed to be taken care of. This was confirmed when, on entering Number 10 one day, both had to squeeze past two bailiffs' men who were carrying out a large escritoire, an event which Pitt himself did not seem to think particularly strange.

'The bailiffs come and go like great turtles, carapaces of furniture upon their backs,' he told her.

'But you are the Prime Minister of England,' she protested, 'and my father says that you are a kind of economic and mathematical genius and that if you hadn't given us a Navy, Napoleon would be in London by now. My father says that when you took over, not much older than I am now, all we had was rotting hulks. Now we have ninety-five ships of the line!'

There was a sweet naivety about her which was captivating and Pitt found himself attracted as never before. She meanwhile became more determined than ever to become part of his life, making sure she got to know every aspect of him. She visited the House of Commons and sat in the Strangers' Gallery watching and listening to him just as he had observed his father. Later she remarked how brutish and obstructive the Opposition were, making things so difficult that it was as though he had to fight them as well as the French.

'It is our system,' he explained, 'I am supposed to sharpen the blade of my intellect upon the whetstone of their criticism. Besides, I've had to do some fearsomely unpopular things to finance this endless war. I, the great tax reducer, have been forced to become the first man in history to put a tax on

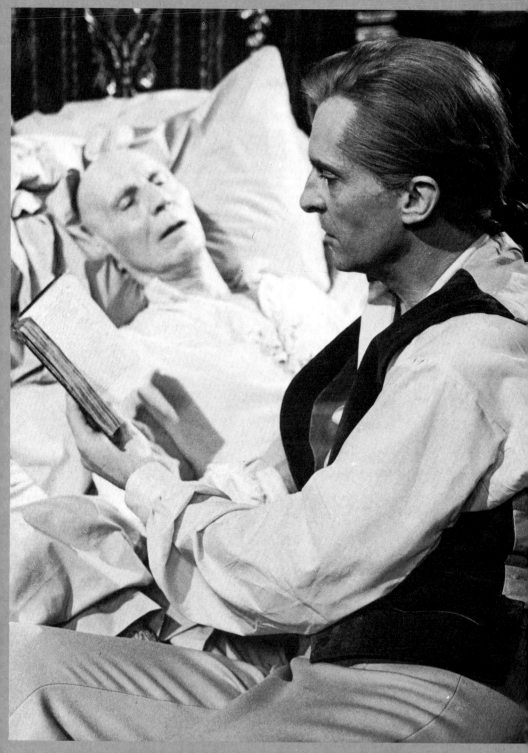

William Pitt the Younger (Jeremy Brett) reading to his dying father, the 1st Earl of Chatham (Alfred Burke)

William Pitt (Jeremy Brett) explaining the finer points of politics to Eleanor Eden (Caroline Langrishe)

The anguished William Pitt (Jeremy Brett) telling his eldest brother, John (Keith Barron), how he is terrified of the dark blood of the Pitts, and the effect that this might have on any children that he were to father

people's incomes. That hurts – the common man does not forget an assault upon his purse.'

Which was something she pointedly said she did not understand, for it seemed to her that the assault had been made on his own purse, from the way he seemed to be in continual debt. When she suggested that she might help him by sorting out his housekeeping expenses, he, indifferent as always to his own personal wealth and economics, happily gave her the freedom to go through what few private accounts he kept. When she had gone back to her parents' home and studied them, she confronted him at their next meeting with facts he did not really want to know.

He was in debt to the tune of £40,000, no less, which she believed was because he had been systematically cheated and defrauded for years. As Prime Minister his salary was £3,780, as Lord of the Treasury £1,220, both of which were already eighteen months in arrears. As Warden of the Cinque Ports he received £3,080, and as Chancellor of the Exchequer £2,452, altogether a total of £10,532, a pretty enough sum. His outgoings, however, were nearly incomprehensible.

His stables the year before had alone cost him £16,000, his bootmaker's bill was £800, which would have to account for a great number of boots. From the butcher's bills it appeared that he had consumed thirty hundredweight of meat during a month when the entire household was away in the country, and in one year it seemed that he had drunk 2,410 bottles of port, 854 bottles of madeira and 572 bottles of claret. Somewhere he was being robbed, or somewhat overdoing things, and, anyway, why had he not accepted the outright gift of £100,000 offered twice by the City of London to remove all worries of this kind?

The answer was simple and obvious, he wanted to be completely free, independent and beholden to no one, answerable only to his country.

Concerned that he looked tired, Eleanor asked him whether he could not go more often to his country house at Holwood as she felt that London oppressed him and that dreadful Downing Street was beginning to weigh him down. But distance was not the only objective that he had for going to Holwood; it also happened to be only five miles from Eleanor's home at Eden Farm, and he was beginning to find his interest in her more than just a fascination for a wide-eyed child.

After he had met her, he had gone to Holwood for a weekend and had stood still at midnight by his bedroom window, fancying that he could see a light in hers shining through the trees. 'You have no idea how wonderfully strangely that affected me, and what a comfort.'

It was as romantic an admission as it was disturbing, for he did not feel he could dispose of his life as he wanted. 'I am the pilot at the centre of the storm and the struggle can be directed only from the heart of power, here in London.'

'So you stay here to have your heart broken by allies who betray you, coalitions of Continental armies, who take England's subsidies and crumble – and malicious men in the House of Commons who care nothing for England, but only to see you fall,' Eleanor pointed out.

Recognizing the perception of her argument, he decided that it would only be right and proper for her to return to the bosom of her family instead of staying in London to be with him, and told her to summon her maid. 'We've been together since the forenoon,' he said. 'If I weren't twice your age people might say I'd compromised you. Come, be off with you!'

At the door of the library they were inevitably drawn closer to each other and they embraced. However much he wanted to deny it, the bachelor Prime Minister was being drawn into a battle in a quite new area of life.

A while later, with the relationship between Eleanor and William progressing, the Prime Minister was called on at Number 10 by his enemy, Charles James Fox. Fox had come to remind him, if he needed reminding, that he was not a man to help him win the war. Pitt had proposed raising income tax to three pence in the pound, and the Opposition leader now made it known that if he did so he would bring Pitt's administration crashing to the ground. Though Bonaparte could not be held back by cardboard soldiers or painted ships, Fox was not interested, his was a private war.

Charles James Fox, the Whig statesman, from a portrait by Hickel

'Mr Fox,' Pitt said, 'I have enough enemies abroad. I do not need more at home. If that is all the help you can extend to me please begone to your mistress, Mrs Armitage, and vex me no more!'

To which Fox replied, 'If the topic is mistresses, Sir, we know what we know!'

Pitt was unsure what was meant, but he was certain that Fox would make something unpleasant of whatever rumour might be going the rounds of the salons.

The war escalated, the Dutch and Spaniards joined Bonaparte and declared war on Britain. When the Austrians made a separate peace with the French, Britain was alone and defenceless. Worse, the fleets at Spithead and the Nore had mutinied and without its Navy, England was a half open door. Already the French had tried to land in Ireland and Wales, and only God and the foul weather had dashed them on the rocks.

At a rare Cabinet meeting Pitt proposed to raise the pay and conditions of the Navy by taxing everything from lace to brandy. He recognized that the people would not like this, but he also knew that they would not like giving up half their bread and meat to stuff the fat bellies of French farmers, which assuredly they would be obliged to do if Bonaparte won.

He did not wait either for a reaction or advice from his ministers but simply got up and left the Cabinet Room after making the announcement. This prompted Castlereagh, his Minister of War, to state, 'Mr Pitt increasingly gives the impression that Cabinet meetings are an irritating interruption to the serious business of running the country,' which led three other ministers, Richmond, Dundas and Canning, to discuss a matter of more immediate concern.

Gossip and Pitt's increasing visits to the country were undermining the Prime Minister's reputation. Though they agreed that a man's private life had always been his own, Pitt's private life was not going to remain so much longer. Everyone was talking about his relationship with the young Eleanor and despite the fact that she was accompanied by her maid during her meetings with Pitt, it was general knowledge that the girl was mostly up in the hay loft with Pitt's ostler. As a chaperone she was about as useful as a 'madame'. Pitt had also permitted her to visit him unaccompanied at Number 10 and, according to Dundas, 'They romped in and out of the place like a couple of bairns.'

Canning thought a little latitude of courtship was acceptable before the plunge into matrimony, but the others were doubtful that marriage was in Pitt's mind. Meanwhile her father, Lord Auckland, was becoming more and more convinced that his pretty young daughter was being misled.

The problem was, of course, that the Prime Minister was skittling with the affections of a girl from a distinguished family. Had she been a scullery maid it would not only have been found perfectly acceptable, but even

'A ministerial mode of paying taxes', a cartoon from 1797 showing Pitt as Prime Minister and First Lord of the Treasury, and Lord Dundas as Secretary of State for War, trying to raise extra taxes to pay for increased naval expenditure in the war against the French

amusing. His ministers were aware that it was an extremely tricky subject and decided to talk to Pitt's elder brother, the Earl of Chatham.

As far as John Pitt was concerned, he found his brother's mind on the subject as difficult to read as a Greek primer. He declared that he believed any interference from anyone in the Cabinet would reduce their chances of remaining in office. In other words, it was really nobody else's business.

The plain fact, as they saw it, was that William Pitt taking a mistress half his age would stick in the nation's craw. It was a tattling tale that could destroy him, the Tory Party and the country and as he was the only man in Europe with the genius to stand up to Bonaparte, there was only one solution and that was for him to marry the girl.

Chatham agreed but warned them that it would not be any simpler for *him* to mention the idea to his brother.

Let me tell you something, gentlemen [he said], I may be older than him by three years. I may have inherited the title. I may have gone to Winchester while he was a sickly lad tutored at home until his doctor put him on a regime of port wine, but the fact is that ever since we grew to be men, he has had the ascendancy. There is something in him that makes him seem more like my father than my younger brother, and there are considerations of which you know nothing; nor could anything prevail upon me to reveal them.

The William-Eleanor relationship went happily on. He visited her in the country, she visited him in Downing Street and took more and more interest in his political life, making it evident that she was not just a romantic female with little in her head.

'You have no need to engage me in what you fondly believe to be woman talk,' she once told him, 'I know what goes on in the wide world. I know, for instance, that you have settled the naval mutinies.'

'With a combination of floggings, glittering sovereigns and a number of Radicals in gaol,' he admitted, 'England has her belt buckled about her again, but King George is gone mad again and is strapped down in Doctor Willis's patent restraining chair, swearing lurid English oaths in a heavy Hanoverian accent.'

This was yet another problem for Pitt – the King was mad. Recently it had become known that he had held a prolonged conversation with a tree in Windsor Great Park under the impression that it was the King of Prussia.

Chatham at last summoned up the courage to talk to his younger brother; which came to nothing but a confirmation that the whole situation was impossible. Pitt would neither give up seeing Eleanor, nor, of course, his office. For a while events forced the lovers apart and Eleanor wrote a pleading letter to her Prime Minister.

My Dearest Will, I cannot bear this enforced separation. I know very well that the King's illness has much pre-occupied you and that affairs of State press upon you and that the war with the obnoxious French goes badly. But you always had much business and yet we found time to be together. For those who love, there is always time, even though it is never enough. Half the summer is gone. I sit here in the country, looking at green meadows. Without you, they are as desolate as the Russian steppes. Could we but have a scant hour together, I could store it away like a squirrel and eke it out in my fancy for weeks and weeks. Please come down soon, Will, oh please! I don't know how much longer I can stand this. All my deepest love, my adored one. Eleanor.

No sooner had he received the letter than she was knocking on the door of Number 10, having told her parents she was going to stay with an aunt. The relationship was turning into passion.

Then it became public.

The *Morning Post* published a cartoon by Gilray which showed Pitt leading Eleanor into a bower in the Garden of Eden with Satan, looking remarkably like Charles James Fox, peeping round a corner of the bushes. The caption read: 'To the nuptial bower he led her, blushing like the morn-

Gilray's cartoon of Pitt leading Eleanor into the nuptial bower in the garden of Eden, with Satan – bearing a remarkable resemblance to Charles James Fox – lurking in the bushes

The nuptial bower with the evil one peeping at the charms of Eden.'

This shook Pitt. 'I have made the loveliest girl in England a butt for the sniggers of louts,' he said guiltily to his brother, who again suggested that there was a perfectly simple and happy remedy – marriage.

But it was the one remedy that was not available to William. He was ill and was taking a number of drugs as well as drinking three bottles of port a day. 'The doctors give me five years before this damned war kills me. A fine prospect to offer a girl.'

He was also too poor to marry, having debts of £45,000 which, Chatham pointed out, could be paid by the City of London if he would only allow it. They were still offering a gift of £100,000. But Pitt would be no man's pensioner.

Chatham, realizing that his brother was more sick than he had thought, tackled the subject head-on and asked him outright if he really loved Eleanor or whether she was just an amusement.

'I love her more passionately than I will ever love anyone or anything in my life,' he answered, 'but I cannot marry her. Never! Never! Never!

And at last the truth came out.

I swore an oath to father as he died. We are of two kinds, we Pitts, two bloods. There's the icy blood of the Grenvilles, which comes from our mother. Then there is the other – the blood of Diamond Jack Pitt, who founded our dynasty. It's a wild blood, unmanageable, unpredictable. It brings genius with it; it also brings strange fancies. An uproar in the mind, a tumult, a heat in the brain. You have the good fortune to be totally Grenville in your temperament, the Pitt strain passed you by. I took it all. Do you remember having to prise my fingers from Crewe's throat? It took four of you to do it. I had every intention of killing him.

Pitt was referring to an occasion when Fox's bully boys, streaming out of Brooks's Club in St James's, had attacked Pitt's carriage and were smashing it to matchwood. The Pitts had decided their only course was to fight their way out. They were rescued by a relief force of young blades from White's Club, fortified by professional pugilist guests; but not before William Pitt, admittedly in self-defence, had nearly strangled Lord Crewe.

What Pitt knew, but nobody else suspected, was that the cool composure, the disdain, the whole bearing he had adopted to set the country to rights was studied, calculated: a fake Grenville masking a Pitt. Whenever he felt the madness come upon him, he drowned it in port. 'Father recognized it and he made me swear that should I find Diamond Jack powerful in me, I would not perpetuate him – ever. The blood is a greedy blood, it feeds grossly on genius. Would you have the Pitts dribble out in a draggle of dolts and idiots?'

The Pitt family history was, in fact, one of great instability. One of the 1st Earl of Chatham's sisters had died in a lunatic asylum, another had died mad at home, four of his brothers were intermittently insane throughout their lives.

'That is what lurks in me,' he explained. 'How can I inflict that on a precious creature like Eleanor Eden? How should I forgive myself if she bore mad things for children?'

Pitt wrote to Eleanor's father, apologizing for the cartoon which had wronged his daughter by making her the subject of vulgar speculation. Eleanor reacted characteristically by calling at Number 10 and demanding an explanation as to why he thought a cartoon implying that they would be married should be injurious.

His answer was painfully blunt. 'We are not going to be married, are we? At least, I do not recollect asking you. I am sorry if you were misled by the natural sympathy that existed between us, our common feeling for Nature, our ease of converse, but you are barely twenty and I am a sick man.'

Not unnaturally she argued. She was what he needed, he had always needed her, he had needed her before she was born and he had always suffered for the want of her. Before her there had been no one, after her there would be no one. She begged him not to destroy them both.

'I shan't destroy you,' he told her gently. 'Life is strong in you. You will

Hoppner's portrait of William Pitt

take another direction and when you are my age you will reflect and be glad that you did.' He then ended the relationship. 'I return to the point from which I started. I never spoke of marriage. It is very simple. I do not wish to marry you.'

It was over.

Eleanor Eden returned to her family and did not venture back to London, or even into Society for some years. Eventually she married Lord Hobart. Pitt gave her husband a place in his government, and she was a frequent visitor with him to Number 10. The record is silent on how she and Pitt behaved or felt when they met again.

Pitt once more threw himself exclusively into the work of saving Britain. In 1801 he resigned over George III's refusal to accept his Catholic Emancipation Bill. But, two years later, war flared up again with France. Napoleon threatened to invade England, and in 1804 the King asked Pitt to head a new administration. With Napoleon sweeping across Europe, the new Prime Minister formed a coalition with Russia, Austro-Hungary and Sweden; Bonaparte was checked at sea by the battle of Trafalgar in July the following year. The Prime Minister, still in his forties, was hailed as the saviour of Europe, but he rightly saw this accolade was premature.

Toasted universally as 'the pilot who weathered the storm', he made his reply very briefly at a Guildhall banquet to which his coach had been pulled by the crowd: 'I return you many thanks for the honour you have done me. But Europe is not to be saved by any single man. England has saved herself by her exertions and will, I trust, save Europe by her example!'

Napoleon fought back, defeated the Austrians and the Russians at the battle of Austerlitz in December. The news of this shattered Pitt. Worn out by his ceaseless efforts of the past twenty-five years, he fell ill.

He was emaciated and weak with gout, the childhood sickness which had never left him. Though at the time doctors knew more about the symptoms of that particular disease than of many others, they were not aware that gout crystallized in the kidneys, leading to renal failure. Nor did they suspect that Pitt's enormous intake of port wine over the years would cause cirrhosis of the liver.

On 23 January 1806, ill in bed and watched over by his doctors and friends, William Pitt, aged forty-six, suddenly sat up in bed: 'D' you know,' he said, referring to his favourite chop-house, just outside the Commons, 'I think I could go one of Bellamy's veal pies.'

Two hours later he died.

CHAPTER THREE

The Iron Duke

D uke of Wellington, Marquis of Douro, Earl Wellington of Somerset, Viscount Wellington of Talavera, Baron Douro of Wellesley, Prince of Waterloo in The Netherlands, Duke of Ciudad Rodrigo in Spain, Duke of Brunoy in France, Duke of Vittoria, Marquis of Torres Vedras, Count of Vimiero in Portugal, a Grandee of the First Class in Spain, a Privy Councillor, Commander-in-Chief of the British Army, Colonel of the Brigadier Guards, Field Marshal of Great Britain, a Marshal of Russia, of Austria, of France, of Prussia, of Spain, of Portugal, of The Netherlands, Knight of the Garter, of the Holy Ghost, of the Golden Fleece, of the Black Eagle, Knight Grand Cross of the Bath, of Hanover, Lord High Constable of England, Constable of the Tower, of Dover Castle, Warden of the Cinque Ports, Chancellor of the University of Oxford. . . .

Referred to by his indifferent mother, the Countess of Mornington, as 'that ugly little boy Arthur', the future Duke of Wellington was born in Dublin on 1 May 1769, the Hon. Arthur Wesley, third surviving son of the 1st Earl of Mornington, a professor of music at Trinity College Dublin, and a composer of sacred music, madrigals and glees. The family were Anglo-Irish aristocrats with a long pedigree. They had two homes, one in Dublin itself and another at Dangan, County Meath, an impressive stone mansion with an organ and harpsichord in the entrance hall, but little else in the other rooms.

Living mainly on a diminishing inherited fortune, Arthur's father was no great financier. In 1781 the whole family moved to London to live in lodgings in Knightsbridge, where the Earl of Mornington promptly died leaving his wife with seven children: Richard, William and Anne, who were older than Arthur; and Gerald, Henry and Mary Elizabeth, who were younger. At his father's death Arthur was twelve and was therefore sent to

Eton, where he showed no aptitude whatsoever for lessons and even less for games which, thankfully for him, were neither organized nor compulsory in those days. Though reputed to have paid his *alma mater* the tribute that 'the Battle of Waterloo was won on the playing fields of Eton', it is very doubtful that he ever said such a thing, or even thought it.

Because his younger brothers, Gerald and Henry, were brighter than him, his mother decided to remove him from the school in order to give them the better education – as a widow she could not afford to keep all three of them there. In 1784, therefore, he spent a while in Brighton with a private tutor, then accompanied his mother to Brussels as she thought it a good idea for him to learn French, and moreover could no longer afford to live in London.

The year in Belgium proved a hardship for her mainly because she discovered her son's principal interest was the violin. Not having been allowed to play it often at Eton, he apparently practised continually in Brussels, where the neighbours seemed to be immune to the noise. Her awkward seventeen-year-old son, she realized, was beginning to pose a problem. Richard, at twenty-six, was already in Parliament, William, twenty-four, was in the Irish House of Commons, Gerald, sixteen, was destined for the Church, and Henry was still too young to be thought about. So, though 'young clumsy Arthur' was not a bit keen on things military, she decided that this should be the career for him. He was duly sent off to a riding academy at Angers in France to prepare him for the Army.

Angers was mainly a riding school, but the pupils were also taught fencing and dancing, and Arthur began to blossom. Rather than attend tedious riding lessons, he was more often engaged in socializing, belonging to an English set known as the 'Groupe des Lords' who were frequent guests at the Duc de Brissac's château, where they were wined and dined in the company of their French contemporaries, Chateaubriand and Talleyrand.

After two years abroad, Lady Mornington, deciding that Arthur was nothing more than 'food for powder', asked Richard to use his influence to find his brother a commission. Richard, then a Junior Lord of the Treasury under the Elder Pitt, made the right noises in the direction of the Lord Lieutenant of Ireland, but had to remind him in writing of his request when nothing had come of them: 'A younger brother of mine, whom you were so kind to take into consideration for the commission, is here at the moment and perfectly idle. It is a matter of indifference to me what commission he gets providing he gets one soon.'

In March 1787 Arthur Wesley received the King's commission as ensign in the Seventy-Third Highland Regiment. But, as the regiment was stationed in India and no one saw any real reason why he should join it, he went on kicking his heels at home. Instead he was dispatched to Dublin,

*Anne, Countess of Mornington, the Duke of Wellington's mother. Lady Mornington
found her son Arthur the source of little maternal satisfaction until his rapid success
in the army*

being transferred initially to the Forty-First Infantry Regiment, and then to the Twelfth Dragoons.

His mother took a brief interest in her eighteen-year-old son now that he had lost his awkwardness and looked rather handsome in his uniform. She expounded her maternal pride in a letter to a friend:

There are so many little things to settle for Arthur who is just got into the army and is to go to Ireland in the capacity of Aide De Camp to Lord Buckingham, and must be set out a little for that, in short I must do everything for him and when you see him you will think him worthy of it as he really is a very charming young man, never did I see such a change for the better in any body, he is wonderfully lucky, in six months he has got two steps in the army and appointed Aide De Camp to Lord Buckingham which is ten shillings a day.

Four years earlier the Act of Union had joined the English and Irish Parliaments, and a wave of natural confidence was sweeping over Ireland, and especially Dublin, where Catholics and Protestants, Whigs and Tories were working together to improve their lot. As in France, young Arthur socialized and was soon noted as the object of much attention from the female section of society, though it was said that some ladies refused to go on picnics if 'that mischievous boy Arthur Wesley' was also to be there.

Arthur was in a good position to be mischievous, for as aide to the Duke of Buckingham at Dublin Castle he had a vantage-point behind the throne to eye the pretty young society things who came to be presented to the Viceroy. He also had the opportunity to spend money, for by 1789, when he had been promoted to lieutenant and Buckingham had been replaced by the Earl of Westmorland, the extravagance at court was compared to that of the Sun King, Louis XIV. No longer able to play the violin because it was an unbecoming pastime for a military man, Arthur had instead taken up cards, and was not too good a gambler.

A new arrival on the scene at about this time was Kitty Pakenham, the second daughter of the Earl of Longford, who lived at Pakenham Hall not thirty miles from Dangan. Arthur had met her before, but now at eighteen she was noticeably attractive and even described as 'an undefinable beauty'. He made up his mind he would marry her.

His brother William had joined Richard in the London Parliament, so to keep a Wesley in a local seat, Arthur stood as the Tory candidate for Trim and was duly elected. He also rose in rank to captain and therefore thought himself a rather good catch. It was somewhat of a surprise, therefore, when his offer of marriage to the young Kitty was turned down, even though he bought further promotions in the Eighteenth Light Dragoons and the Thirty-Third Foot, using a loan from his brother, Richard. Kitty Pakenham, well-bred and polite, said goodbye to him.

Instead the rejected Arthur turned his attention to what was happen-

Kitty Pakenham, Duchess of Wellington, from a portrait by Sir Thomas Lawrence

ing on the Continent which, though a good deal less pleasant, might prove more fulfilling. In 1789 France had exploded into revolution. On 21 January 1793 Louis XVI had been guillotined and England, Holland, Spain, Portugal, Tuscany, Naples and the Holy Roman Empire united to fight the warring French.

Arthur, content to make soldiering his life, took his first serious steps towards his glorious career. With the rank of lieutenant colonel he was put in command of a brigade and sent to Flanders, where he fought a rearguard action with great coolness, learning 'how things should not be done'.

Returning home to Ireland, he found the pressure of politics and of his debts unfavourable, so in 1795 he decided to go to the West Indies with the Thirty-Third Foot. Instead, the regiment was sent to India, a land that was suffering both from the expanding and corrupt activities of greedy European traders and from the warring states of the Mahrattas.

In 1600 Elizabeth I had established the Honourable East India Company. Robert Clive, a hundred and fifty years later, further helped to lay its foundations of power in the Indian subcontinent, but by the late 1700s the Company was proving itself far from honourable. From its Court of Directors in London to the network of civil servants and military personnel in Bengal, Bombay and Madras, all were hell bent on making a fortune. But now that war had broken out in Europe, it became obvious that the French, who had been passive rival traders, could pose a threat, and so the British had to strengthen their position by subduing the Mahrattas and getting control of one or more of their princely states.

Within the year three Wesley brothers were in India: Arthur; Richard, 2nd Earl of Mornington, who arrived as Governor General; and Henry, who acted as his secretary. Because the family were rising in status, Richard decided to re-adopt the ancestral family name of Wellesley with its 'ampler air', and from May 1798, when he took up his appointment in Madras, all of them became known by that name.

Arthur Wellesley was dispatched to Mysore to deal with Typoo Sahib who had drawn up an alliance with the French. He dealt admirably with him and did further excellent work throughout the Seringapatam expedition, taking over the subsequent administration of the newly acquired territory. The Mahrattas broke down after victorious battles at Ahmednagar and Assaye, and the final defeat of the enemy at Argaum. Arthur was knighted and received a fortune amounting to £40,000: 'Enough,' as he said, 'to make me independent, but not a Nabob.'

He had learned to live under canvas for three years, to remain in the saddle for hour after hour, and to train unpromising men to become dependable soldiers. The distance his troops marched was unprecedented, in military terms he was a record breaker, and he had invented a wheel to measure the foot-miles covered by his men, a device that preceded the

Hoppner's portrait of Major-General the Hon. Sir Arthur Wellesley on military service in India

leading platoon and on which he calculated what could be done without exhaustion.

Now, after nine years, he returned to Ireland as Sir Arthur Wellesley, not rich in comparison to other people, but very much so in comparison with his former situation, and quite sufficiently for his own wants. Though neither he nor Kitty Pakenham had corresponded once with each other during all the time he was away, he looked forward to meeting her again. Warned that she was not as pretty as she had been, he remarked on seeing her again that 'she had grown ugly, by Jove', but they took up where they had left off. Now an eligible bachelor, he was also described by a contemporary as handsome, very brown, quite bald and with a hooked nose. He was not bald at all but had his head closely shaved in order to wear a fashionable wig on certain occasions.

The strange romance between these two who outwardly did not show too many signs of love, was commented on so much in Society that even Queen Charlotte asked Kitty, when she was at Court, if it was true that she had never written to her lover when he was abroad.

'No never Madame,' Kitty answered.

'And did you never think of him?'

'Yes Madame, very often.'

They were married, but apart from staying a few days longer than his leave permitted, Arthur did little to make his new wife feel wanted, travelling back to England alone, while she followed later with her brother. About the occasion he later wrote, 'I married her because they asked me to do it and I did not know myself. I thought I should never care for anybody again and that I should be with my army and, in short, I was a fool.'

After he was posted to Hastings there followed a period of various military and civil duties. Asked whether it wasn't too quiet for him after India he replied 'I am Nimmukwallah, as they say in India. I have ate of the King's salt and therefore I conceive it to be my duty to serve with unhesitating zeal and cheerfulness when and wherever the King or his government may think proper to employ me.'

The Whigs, under Lord Grenville, were in government and it was unlikely that a worthwhile appointment would come Arthur's way. Not that he was lamenting his position, for he had a lucrative command and this was making him rich.

In 1806 he was elected Member of Parliament for Rye in Sussex, and then, in the first weeks of 1807, for Mitchell (St Michael and Michael Midshall) in Cornwall, a seat he relinquished several months later for Newport on the Isle of Wight. Kitty, now a frail woman of thirty-six, gave birth to their first son, Arthur Richard, during the same year. The father of the child was no great help to her, treating her much as he might have a wounded soldier in the field. She, in fact, got very little sympathy from him on any front, for when coping with a disaster at home – a maid committed suicide after being crossed in love by the head gardener – he wrote to her, 'I hope the remainder of the maids will put up with misfortunes of this world and not destroy themselves. Let the gardener be taken back. It is evident that he had nothing to say to the death of this woman.'

In 1807 there was a change of government. The Duke of Portland became Prime Minister and Sir Arthur was invited to accept the post of Chief Secretary for Ireland, which he took up at Dublin Castle. Deprived by the Act of Union of the traditional leadership of its landed gentry, the country was turning to more exciting revolutionary substitutes. Sir Arthur Wellesley wrote to his government:

No political measure which you could adopt would alter the temper of the people of this country. They are disaffected to the British Government; they don't feel the benefits of their situation; attempts to render it better either do not reach their minds, or they are represented to them as additional injuries; and in fact we have no strength here but the army. Ireland has been kept connected with Great Britain by the distinction between Protestants and Catholics since the Act of Settlement. The Protestants were the English garrison. Abolish the distinction and all will be Irishmen alike, with similar Irish feelings. Show me an Irishman and I'll show you a man whose anxious wish it is to see his country independent of Great Britain.

Independence was what the Irish wanted and Sir Arthur Wellesley was against giving them any more. He advised to keep them down by force, for they had too much power and would only use more to obtain more.

In September 1807 Napoleon had decreed the closure of all Continental ports to British trade, and the surrender of the neutral Portuguese and Danish fleets. It was clear that the French Emperor was planning to use the Danish ships anchored in Copenhagen to invade England. Canning, the Foreign Minister, therefore ordered Denmark to place its fleet at Britain's disposal. Denmark refused, so the British set sail with a task force and Sir Arthur Wellesley in charge of a brigade. He landed with an advance guard not far from Copenhagen, the army followed and the city was surrounded. Ten days later, during the siege, a Danish relief army loomed on the horizon and Sir Arthur was told to cut it off. He did this with such expertise that no further attempts were made to relieve the city and Wellesley only lost a hundred and seventy-two men, though the Danes fared worse. On his return he was publicly thanked for his genius, valour, intrepidity and exertion.

In 1808 Kitty gave birth to a second son, but Sir Arthur, now the youngest lieutenant general in the British Army, was more interested in taking another crack at Napoleon, who had invaded Portugal.

Early in May, Ferdinand VII of Spain, who had been put on the throne by the people after his unpopular father had been deposed, was summoned to

Goya's sketch in chalk of the Duke of Wellington, drawn in Madrid in 1812

Bayonne by Napoleon. There he forced him to abdicate in favour of Joseph Bonaparte. Patriotic Spain rose in fury and sent a deputation to England, followed by a similar deputation from Portugal, urging joint attacks on the common enemy. Napoleon, it was agreed, had to be checked, and a delighted Sir Arthur was sent to the Iberian peninsula.

Between 1808 and 1814, he was in Spain fighting the French Army, maintaining throughout a tactical defensive position within a strategical offensive until his opponents, ill-nourished and badly-organized due to vulnerable supply lines, were sufficiently disrupted and worn down to be attacked with complete confidence. The battles of Talavera in 1809 and Salamanca in 1812 showed the supremacy of the British with their Portuguese and German allies, and though there were setbacks, the French were eventually driven out of Spain and brought to submission at Toulouse. Napoleon was sent into exile on the island of Elba.

Sir Arthur Wellesley was created Knight Grand Cross of the Order of the Bath, became Field Marshal the Duke of Wellington, Knight of the Order of the Garter, the recipient of many distinguished foreign orders, and was awarded £400,000 by the House of Commons.

In 1814 he was appointed Ambassador in Paris and on arriving there bought as an embassy a suitably spacious house in the Rue du Faubourg St Honoré which had belonged to the Borghese family. The Paris season of 1814 was an endless party. Half fashionable London was there and the new and glamorous Ambassador was surrounded by the gay, the pretty and the successful. While Kitty remained in England, the Duke enjoyed the company of his female devotees, among them Lady Caroline Lamb without her poet lover Byron, and Harriet Arbuthnot, wife of Wellington's lifelong friend at the Treasury, Charles Arbuthnot.

On 1 November 1814 the Congress of Vienna opened, where representatives of all the powers of Europe assembled to settle the new frontiers. Wellington joined the Congress in the following February, but a month later hurriedly left on hearing that Napoleon had escaped from the island of Elba.

Matters quickly came to a head: Napoleon landed in France, marched on Paris and entered the Tuileries; allied armies were assembled under Wellington; Napoleon with his army crossed the Belgian frontier, and on 18 June met Wellington to do battle.

His wife Kitty, in a quite uncharacteristic stroke of prescience, had said, 'If Arthur ever meets that man [Napoleon], he will destroy him at a stroke.'

The Battle of Waterloo ended the war.

The victorious Duke, Commander-in-Chief of the allied army of occupation, returned to London in 1817 to be presented by the nation with

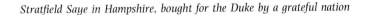

Stratfield Saye in Hampshire, bought for the Duke by a grateful nation

Apsley House, Number 1 Piccadilly, the London home of the Duke of Wellington

Stratfield Saye, a vast estate in Hampshire. He also bought himself a London residence, Apsley House at Hyde Park Corner, known as No 1 Piccadilly.

For the first time in many years he was home, but to a man who had moved from Eton to Brussels, Angers, Dublin and India, had spent six years in the field in Spain, lived in the Paris Embassy in grand luxury before fighting one of history's most important battles, home was a little hard to define. He had his two huge houses but hardly felt comfortable in either of them. They were run by the disorganized Kitty who fluttered between the two and invited a multitude of guests that he didn't really want to see and that she hardly ever recognized due to short-sightedness. More often than not the Duke was to be found cosily settled in his own chair at the Arbuthnots' house in Parliament Street, where he found the peace he needed.

He had first met Harriet Arbuthnot in Paris and though she was a hand-some woman, he had been surrounded by prettier ones. But she was more intelligent than most and she listened well. With her he could talk politics and, more important, trust her to keep what they discussed to herself. Harriet did not gush, she knew how to behave with him in public and stood no nonsense from him in private. She was bossy, which was a change for the dominating Duke, and he soon nicknamed her 'La Tirana', referring to

The Duke walking in the park with Harriet Arbuthnot

Harriet Wilson, the courtesan who threatened to reveal her relationship with the Duke of Wellington

himself as 'her Slave'. It was a common joke enjoyed by all, including Charles Arbuthnot, an invaluable subordinate who, working at the Treasury, had an unlimited source of official knowledge at his finger tips. There is a halfway house between love and friendship, Wellington thought, more precious than either, but harder to maintain. This is what he believed they all shared.

In 1818 Wellington became Master General of Ordnance in Lord Liverpool's Tory administration and remained in the Cabinet for the next eight years. It was during this time that he received a letter from a publisher of scandalous pornographic books in Paris.

My Lord Duke, In Harriet Wilson's Memoirs, which I am about to publish, are various anecdotes of your Grace which it would be most desirable to withhold, at least such is my opinion. I have stopped the Press for the moment; but as the publication will take place next week, little delay can necessarily take place. I have the honour to be, My Lord Duke, Your Grace's ever attached Servant.

The Duke had visited Harriet Wilson, London's most aspiring courtesan, in the early 1790s, and had been entertained by her on many occasions. She boasted having kept company with all the dandies of the period, from Sheridan to Beau Brummel, and obviously her memoirs would prove delicious reading.

Wellington's reply to the suggestion of blackmail has in fact been lost, but legend has it that he dealt with the problem by scrawling his answer in flaming red ink across the publisher's letter – an answer which is now part of the English language – PUBLISH AND BE DAMNED!

In August 1827 George Canning, who had succeeded Lord Liverpool as Prime Minister, died after being in office barely three months. It was expected that the Duke, a staunch Tory, would take over. His political policy was to refrain from weakening established authority and avoid foreign entanglements. He was a man who took decisions, knew what he wanted and had had enough experience of commanding armies to get his way. But George IV wanted someone more flexible, so Lord Goderich was appointed instead.

Lord Goderich, however, proved too weak; so weak in fact that he often burst into tears when things went wrong. Finally the King had to withdraw his support and ask the Duke to form a government after all. On 8 January 1828, Wellington became Prime Minister and moved into Number 10.

It was taken for granted that he would be a successful premier: he had been in the Cabinet for several years and had never yet failed in anything he had taken on. But he was soon to discover that the difference between ministers and army officers was that the former, when not in agreement with the man in command, could be petulant or even resign.

One man wants one thing and one another [he wrote]. They agree to what I say in the morning, and then in the evening up they start with some crotchet which deranges the whole plan. I have not been used to that in all the early part of my life. I have been accustomed to carry on things in quite a different manner: I assembled my officers and laid down my plan, and it was carried into effect without any more words.

Fifty-nine years old, silver-haired, five foot nine in his Wellington boots, trim, slim and immaculately dressed in dark blue frock coat, white waistcoat, white trousers, white silk cravat and shallow black tricorne hat, the Duke arrived to take possession of his official residence astride his famous chestnut horse Copenhagen, cheered by a large crowd and leading a procession of three heavily laden bullock carts – he organized the removal of his own furnishings. Bullock carts had been his main means of transport in all his campaigns. The movement of supplies across countries, however slow, had thus been reliable, and he saw no reason why he should abandon this method now. He didn't like the cheering. He characterized it as 'an expression of opinion from the mob. Once you let the mob show approval, you open the door to their showing disapproval at another time.'

Among the items moved into Number 10 was his extremely narrow camp bed, on which he had slept throughout his campaigns. On being asked how on earth he managed to turn over on it, he replied: 'When it's time to turn over, it's time to turn out.'

Waiting to settle him into the house were his friends Harriet and Charles Arbuthnot. It was to them he turned for efficient household organization, not Kitty, whom he preferred to keep at a distance in Hampshire at Stratfield Saye. Besides, he could talk over his problems with the Arbuthnots, who understood completely the subtleties and nuances of political manoeuvring which would now be his new life, as well as any personal problems. One of these was irritating him at the moment, and threatened to involve them too.

His nephew, William Long-Wellesley, who had served under him in the army, had squandered his wife's fortune and then abandoned her and his three children, running off with a fellow officer's wife. The shock had killed his wife and now he was trying to get possession of his three children because the eldest boy was about to come into a trust fund.

Wellington had made the children wards of court to keep them out of his nephew's clutches until he could legally adopt them himself. But he knew that Long-Wellesley's plan would be to prove him as depraved as himself by painting a lurid picture of his relationship with Harriet and Charles, in which case the courts would award the children to their natural father.

The Duke, however, was not a man to lose sleep over such matters; instead, he directed his energies to the discussions at his first Cabinet meeting, which became heated over the complex question of Catholic Eman-

Copenhagen, the Duke's famous chestnut horse, from a painting by Haydon. His lady friends deemed it a great privilege to be allowed to ride it

cipation in Ireland. He was concerned that people might think him prejudiced, and he wanted it known that he had nothing against Catholicism. In Spain he had given orders to his troops that they were to uncover whenever the Host passed in the streets. He had thought it politic. To those of his men who were Catholics he had given open permission for them to go to mass as often as they wished, resulting in no one grumbling and nobody bothering to go. But Palmerston, Secretary for War, did not think a comparison could be made between the Irish Catholics and his troops in Spain. Whatever the English Catholics might feel, the Irish were unlikely to tolerate any of that religion being disbarred from sitting in Parliament much longer. The Catholic Associations, which Wellington regarded as guerillas with a respectable name, were active again. In his view the sting could be drawn from them by recognizing them, but it was pointed out that the Associations were now being led by the formidable Daniel O'Connell, a man of reason, of great power and intellect.

Wellington was not currently disposed to be exercised about this. When told that times were changing and the Kildare Club in Dublin had admitted the bishops to membership, he replied: 'The Kildare Club can do what they like, but if they have let the Bishops in, they had best look to their umbrellas!'

Meanwhile, more immediately urgent was the fact that the Opposition were making much of electoral reform, and demanding that the right to vote should be extended to the majority. A debate was set in the House for the redistribution of seats in East Retford. The Opposition wanted them to go to the city of Birmingham, to the shopkeepers and artisans, whereas Wellington advocated that they should go to the county of Nottingham where, he reasoned, the landowners would vote in the interest of the country, not in their own. In Wellington's opinion the common man was best off in the hands of his betters. There wasn't one man in his army who wasn't the most villainous scoundrel in his village, yet, forged by him, they had conquered Europe!

But, unlike the Duke, the members of his Cabinet could see that the movement towards greater democracy was inevitable. The mood of England was for the people, and even Percy Bysshe Shelley had written a poem awakening the rebel streak in the populace:

Men of England wherefore plough
For the Lords who laid ye low?
Wherefore weave with toil and care
The rich robes your tyrants wear?

These seemed to be dangerous times, for the French Revolution of 1789 had remained firmly in everyone's memory. George IV, though suffering under several delusions, including an obsession that he had fought at the Battle of Waterloo and at Salamanca, disguised as General Buco, was no fool. He recognized that democratic ideas had led to the outbreak of the Revolution, and then to the Terror, to Bonaparte, and to the sack and ruin of Europe. Both he and his Prime Minister felt it was time to be cautious.

Despite these enormous problems, life at Number 10 was one of fun and games, played hard by both adults and children. The Duke was very fond of children and as war had deprived him of playing with his own sons, he ensured they were very much part of life at Downing Street.

He often carried small change on him, tied up in red or blue ribbons to give to the poorer children he met. 'Are you for the Army or the Navy?' he would ask, and a promising soldier would get a shilling or two done up in red while a likely sailor would get a similar amount tied up in blue. On one occasion he made the error of asking a small person what he would like to be, and received a reproachful response, 'I am a girl, Mr Dook.' So he gave her a red and a blue ribbon with the money, suggesting she should give them both to her beau.

Some visitors to Number 10 were embarrassed to find the Prime Minister on all fours under a table, clearly imagining himself to be his own horse Copenhagen or some other beast in a child's fantasy. Others found themselves the audience to a re-enactment of the battle of Waterloo with

Wellington playing with his grandchildren in the library at Stratfield Saye, Painting by R. Thorburn

Marshal Ney, and Prince Blücher in the shape of seven and twelve year olds. Lady Caroline Lamb was often at the Duke's side on such occasions, joining in the battles and hurling herself at the Duke with screams and laughter. On one occasion she became entangled indelicately on the floor with the Duke's limbs, at the very moment that the butler came in to announce the presence of Mr Huskisson, the Colonial Secretary – one of the 'damned democrats' in the Cabinet – on a matter most urgent.

The House had just divided on the redistribution of the East Retford seats and Huskisson had come to tell His Grace that he had voted with the Opposition: a matter of conscience, a promise given months before the Duke had taken office. In the circumstances he thought it only proper to offer his resignation.

'I accept it,' the Duke said with little ceremony.

This came as a shock to Huskisson, for it had only been a diplomatic suggestion, not a deeply felt conviction.

'You don't understand,' he stammered.

'I understand perfectly well,' the Duke went on. 'A gentleman does not offer his resignation unless he means it. You have resigned, I accept your resignation.'

Harriet Arbuthnot (Gabrielle Drake), the Duke's devoted friend

The Duke of Wellington (Bernard Archard) supervising children's games at Number 10. (The children are, from left to right, Jilly Barker, Rupert Copeman-Hill, Debra Langerman, Rachel Fozzard and Benjamin Barker)

The Duke (Bernard Archard) prepares to duel with Lord Winchilsea on Battersea Fields

'It was a misjudgement on my part, a mistake,' Huskisson protested.

'There is no mistake, there can be no mistake and there shall be no mistake,' the Duke reaffirmed.

But did the Prime Minister realize that if he went so would Palmerston and the other members of the Cabinet?

'Then I shall have to soldier on without you. Goodnight, Huskisson and goodbye,' said the Duke.

After which he happily returned to the drawing room to announce the good news to his friends that he had got rid of the damned democrats at one stroke. 'They exposed a flank to me and I rolled them up!'

A while later the games were again interrupted by the butler, announcing the arrival of Mr William Long-Wellesley, who was apparently offering violence. The Duke decided to see him in his study.

William Long-Wellesley was a big man in his late thirties who instantly threatened the smaller Wellington with a silver-handed sword-stick.

'I've come here to kill you,' he announced.

'I've had a hundred thousand men at a time trying to do that,' Wellington replied.

'None with a motive that speaks so loud as mine. You have deprived me of my children!'

Which was not of course true. Long-Wellesley had deprived himself of them when he had abandoned them without a penny in Italy and run off with another man's wife whom he had seduced by climbing through a window. The Duke knew all the details because he had brought the mother and children home and it had been her dying wish that the children's father should never get his hands on them again. It was therefore the Duke's intention to honour her wish.

Long-Wellesley said he knew that his children were in Hampshire with two aunts and told the Duke that he was going to get them.

'Have a care,' Wellington warned. 'By order of the court I am their legal guardian. I will protect them against you and all mankind.'

'And who will protect you?' Long-Wellesley asked.

In the limited area of the study he then unsheathed a sword from his stick and pressed the point against the Duke's throat. The man was mad, the moment was dangerous, but the Duke was not concerned for his own safety.

'Wellesley,' he said, 'for thirty years I have faced the most practised killers in the world. Do you really suppose you can affright me with your stick pin? Thrust that point an inch further and the gallows rope is around your neck.'

Long-Wellesley was incensed and accused the Duke of wanting to get his own hands on the children's inheritance, and he was still determined to kill him.

'My country has made me one of the richest men in Europe,' Wellington pointed out. 'You attribute your own motives to me, sir. You are a scoundrel, a blackguard, a libertine, a gambler and a wastrel. Even if your wife had not asked me, I would have done all in my power to remove your children from your influence.'

Long-Wellesley, going quite berserk, brought his sword down hard on a piece of furniture, which alarmed the servants who were outside in the hall listening at the door and waiting armed with cudgels to protect their master.

'I shall appeal to the courts and I warn you I shall use every weapon that malice can devise to bring you down,' he ranted.

'I am prepared for that,' Wellington replied. 'Now let me tell you my plan. I will adopt your children and bring them up as my own, with my own. . . .'

Which sent Long-Wellesley into a further rage, hitting out at more furniture with his sword.

Wellington waited patiently for the caprice to subside, then opened the door and asked his butler to see Mr Long-Wellesley out.

Quite unperturbed Wellington then rejoined the children and his female guests in the drawing room where, after allowing them some show of admiration, he started boring them with yet another explanation of one of his inventions, a subject that he tended to go on about whenever the opportunity arose. Had his visitor turned nastier, he had to hand an umbrella from which a lethal blade could be sprung for purposes of self defence against maniacs such as his nephew.

For the Duke was an inventor, and no one came to call without being shown his latest idea, be it a new type of finger bandage, a teapot so balanced in a cradle that it could be tilted to pour without moving it, strange cloaks and mufflers of special design, and even his waterproof boots. 'I always have something up my sleeve,' he explained '– like the dip in the ground at Waterloo.'

Following the resignation of his Cabinet, Wellington appointed his second Cabinet which was more military in content: Charles Arbuthnot was made Chancellor of the Duchy of Lancaster; General Sir George Murray, who had been with him in Spain, was appointed Colonial Secretary; Sir Henry Hardinge, his liaison officer at Waterloo, was made Secretary of War; Lord Fitzgerald became President of the Board of Trade; and Sir Robert Peel was appointed Home Secretary and Leader of the House.

Hardinge suggested uneasily that they might be called the 'Regimental Cabinet', which did not displease the Duke at all.

I've been in Government for thirteen years, as Master of the Ordnance, and I've watched politicians at work. Bunch of recruits with two left feet. I asked the Treasury the other day to make a change in one of their accounting systems.

A risqué cartoon of the Duke of Wellington as Master of the Ordnance

'Impossible' said they. 'Can't be done!' 'Then I'll send in six Pay Corps sergeants to do it for you!' I said. The thing was done within twenty-four hours. Now then, first subject for discussion – Catholic Emancipation. Burdett's Bill recommending it is before the Commons at this moment, I expect it to be rejected. . . .'

On which subject Sir Robert Peel begged to differ as he thought the bill would scrape through. Furthermore, he thought it a tactical error to have appointed Lord Fitzgerald to the Cabinet because, according to the rules, his appointment would force him to put himself up for re-election for the Irish constituency of Clare, and Daniel O'Connell would be standing against him.

'O'Connell's a Catholic, he's not allowed to stand,' Wellington objected.

'Though he's not permitted as a Catholic to sit in Parliament, there's nothing to stop him standing for election to it,' Peel answered.

The Commons passed Sir Francis's Burdett's Bill granting Catholic Emancipation by a majority of six. Murray thought it a straw in the wind, but Wellington considered that that was the place for straw – in the wind, not in the councils of Government. He would have it rectified by the Lords. But it was a growing movement, a tide, and a while later Sir Robert Peel, back from Ireland, called at Number 10 with the news that he had never witnessed such an election. The whole countryside had rallied to O'Connell. Flags and banners were marched through the streets, thousands had camped out in the open overnight so as not to miss his speeches, yet no man had lifted a hand in violence because O'Connell had forbidden it.

Catholic priests had led their flocks in regimented columns to the polling booths, perfect order had prevailed. It had been an exhibition of sober and desperate enthusiasm resulting in O'Connell winning by an avalanche and Fitzgerald losing his seat. Now O'Connell was threatening to come thundering on the doors of Westminster to demand admittance. The tide that had been expected earlier in the year had now become a flood. In Peel's opinion if the Catholics were not emancipated the country could be plunged into civil war.

The Duke needed a little time to think things out.

If political matters were beginning to get on top of him, for the moment he showed no signs of worrying privately. Kitty, living at Stratfield Saye and only to visit Number 10 on a very few occasions, was not one of his problems. Children had priority in his life and he found time for them whenever he thought necessary. Harriet Arbuthnot, who had become his unofficial social secretary, worried about his spending so much valuable time on them. Between Cabinet meetings he once visited one of his many godchildren who was at a day school in Kensington. Her parents were not so rich and in consequence her class-mates were being high-nosed with her. 'I took her a bunch of flowers,' he explained. 'Delivered them personally. Let them be grand with her now!'

He also wrote countless letters to his little friends, one a long history about a toad to a boy who had to go away leaving his pet toad behind. The Duke promised to look after it and sent him regular reports.

'Arthur,' Harriet warned, 'you really must spare yourself. No wonder you suffer from colds. You should clear the house of all these people, the comings and goings and the children.'

But the Duke couldn't do that. 'Remember, I've lived the best part of my life in the army, in the mess, my bright sparks about me. I can't exist in stillness.'

And stillness was about the last thing Number 10 would experience that particular evening, for his 'hareem', as Harriet Arbuthnot called it, was coming to dine.

One of the Duke's favourite pastimes was a boisterous adult game of his own invention which was played down the polished floor of the corridor leading from the entrance hall of Number 10 to the reception area. It consisted of one lady guest, preferably young and pretty, sitting on a tough Persian rug to which was stitched an equally tough leather harness, rather like those used to teach babies to walk.

Strapped into the harness would be any male participant, from Welling-

The APOSTATES and the EXTINGUISHER — or — KISSING the POPE's TOE!!

A cartoon attacking Wellington and Peel for their 'apostacy' concerning Catholic Emancipation. Wellington is shown kissing the Pope's toe, while Peel offers him the crown of the Protestant kingdom

ton himself to the Prince of The Netherlands, or a grandee of Spain, or a Cabinet Minister. The lady would whip the 'horse' with a beribboned riding crop, and the 'horse' would then have to pull the carpet and its occupant as fast as possible down the length of the corridor. The winner was the horse and rider who were the quickest down the track, and betting was by no means forbidden.

During that particular evening's race meeting, with certain of his ministers urging a willing steed, Wellington suddenly called a Cabinet meeting.

'You're to keep quiet for now,' he announced when the Cabinet Room doors were closed and he was alone with his men, 'but I thought I should let you know that I have decided to let the Catholics in. I have made the most rigorous enquiries since Peel's report and I am satisfied he is right. To refuse them would mean a civil war and I will not have that.'

'You would win it hands down,' he was told.

'I would not fight such a war,' he replied; 'it is too horrible to contemplate.'

'The people will call you the greatest turncoat and coward in the history

86

of the kingdom,' Murray told him, to which the Duke replied, 'Then I shall have to bear it, for their sake.'

Having risked his life for years as a soldier and faced the possibility of being murdered by his enraged nephew, he was now to get close to death again in a duel over his decision on Catholic Emancipation.

The Tory Lord Winchilsea, furious at the news that Wellington was going to allow the Relief Bill, demanded to see the Prime Minister and, incensed, reported that the party was in an uproar. 'They have always believed you were the Great Protestant! And you've been damnably sly about it. You and Peel have evidently been working on this for weeks, getting round the King, tickling him like a trout till you've landed him on your side.'

Wellington protested that His Majesty had the right to first knowledge of his Prime Minister's thoughts.

'Dammit, sir, the Party feels betrayed and I've taken it upon myself to tell you so.' Winchilsea ranted. 'You came in as the iron champion of the English Protestant Constitution, now you intend to swamp us in Roman fripperies and wafer cakes! I believe you to be in the pay of the Pope!'

'What would you have me do?' Wellington asked, 'fight a battle that cannot be won? Bring down the Government and let in the Opposition, in which case the Catholics would be admitted anyway? I would have lost everything and gained nothing. This way we steal the Opposition's clothes and stay in power.'

But Winchilsea had bad news. The Duke of Cumberland, the King's brother and a fanatical, die-hard hater of Catholicism almost to the point of madness, who was thought to be snowed up in Germany, had managed to get to England and was to dine with His Majesty that night in order to cleanse the monarch's mind of Popish sophistry. Worse, as Wellington was to learn from Charles Arbuthnot, his nephew Long-Wellesley had just had scurrilous pieces published in a penny magazine which claimed, among other things, that the Long sisters, to whom he had given charge of the children, had taken into service two prostitutes as governesses for them, that one of the sisters was committing incest with her own uncle and that the sisters themselves had a libidinous relationship with each other.

'I'm surprised he left out the sheep and the goats,' Wellington remarked, 'The fellow should be a French novelist.'

But Arbuthnot had not finished. The scandal sheet further stated that Harriet was the Duke's mistress and had been for years.

This, Wellington did not like.

Whatever else, he did not want his friendship with the couple spoilt and he emphasized that Long-Wellesley was only trying to discredit him in the eyes of the Court. Arbuthnot was not personally upset, but was worried about the effect of the scandal on the minds of the public. The word was already on the streets about Catholic Emancipation. It was being said that the Prime Minister would let rich Irish Catholics into Parliament, but would not give poor Protestant Englishmen the vote. The Bishop of Salisbury, said Arbuthnot, had also been active with his pen against Emancipation. He carried great weight.

'Bugger the Bishop of Salisbury!' said Wellington. 'I will have my bill!'

'You are not popular,' Arbuthnot said.

'Popularity is for pugilists and jockeys,' Wellington replied, and proved that he believed it by opposing the King when George IV decided to change his mind and take his brother's advice to stop the Catholics coming in.

'I have resigned,' he told Harriet and Charles calmly on returning from Windsor a few days later, 'So has Peel. So has the whole Cabinet. A feint. A retreat to victory. The King was quite impossible.' And he went on to describe the fearful meeting.

The King had had nothing to eat and he did not offer us anything. For six hours he sat there, drinking brandy and water. He used his customary tactic of talking interminably about anything other than the subject in hand. I employed my usual tactic of letting him talk himself to a standstill. Then I brought up the subject, which he could no longer avoid. Peel was magnificent, I was, I think, tolerably persuasive. The King turned us down, we resigned and left.

'I don't see how you can claim a victory,' Harriet protested.

'Dear Harriet,' the Duke said, 'he cannot do without us. Who else can he turn to? The Opposition Whigs? He believes they would be preparing a republican revolution within a month.'

Though this was not true, Wellington knew that it was what the King believed, and he was banking on this wrong assumption.

Later, the following night, after a long day of agonized waiting, a special courier came from His Majesty with a letter for the Duke.

My Dear Friend, As I have found the country would be left without an Administration, I have decided to yield my opinions to that which is considered by the Cabinet to be for the immediate interests of the country. Let them proceed as proposed with their measure. Postscript: God knows what pain it costs me to write these words. George Rex.

Wellington was not jubilant. He, too, knew what it had cost. As he said, 'There's only one thing as sad as a battle lost and that's a battle won.'

When Wellington had become Prime Minister he had been the most popular man in England. Eighteen months later he was the most hated. He was labelled the Anti-Christ, and a new joke went the rounds that his policy was, 'My Lords! Attention! Right about face! Quick march!'

Though the campaign of lies against him affected only the simple minded, he was aware that they were the majority and he was worried that it could affect the bill.

The Bishop of Salisbury had written in a newspaper that he feared that Catholic Emancipation would undermine the established Church, Long-Wellesley had published a so-called list of the Duke's lady lovers in another scandal sheet called *The Frolicsome Companion*, and now he learned that Lord Winchilsea in *The Standard* had publicly accused him of lying in his speech upholding the teachings of the Protestant faith at King's College, London. 'It is a blind behind which the noble Duke might more effectually, under the cloak of zeal for the Protestant religion, carry on his insidious designs for the infringement of our liberties and the introduction of Popery into every department of the State.'

That settled it for the Duke of Wellington.

There was only one way to stop the man and that was by a duel. If he let this insult pass he would lose his honour and any influence he had in the country.

During the whole of his time in the Army he had expressly forbidden duelling among his officers because he did not see any reason why his officers should do the enemy's job for them, but this was different.

He wrote Winchilsea a note explaining his reasons and ending, 'I now call upon your Lordship to give me that satisfaction for your conduct which a gentleman has a right to require and that a gentleman never refuses to give.' He asked Hardinge, the Secretary of War, to be his second and to get his doctor to meet them at Battersea Fields at a quarter to seven the next morning with a case of pistols.

The next day at dawn on Battersea Fields, Wellington met Hardinge and the doctor. Everyone but the Duke was extremely nervous, for though Wellington planned to aim to miss Winchilsea, he had the reputation of being a formidably bad shot. At a recent pheasant shoot at Lord Granville's he had bagged a gamekeeper, a beater, a village woman hanging out her washing and put nine pellets in Granville's cheek.

The day augured badly.

A carriage and pair arrived a little late and Lord Falmouth, Winchilsea's second, got out, obviously in a high state of nerves. The one-armed Hardinge had some difficulty in loading Wellington's pistol. Falmouth was trembling so much that he fared little better with Winchilsea's. Both seconds made a last-minute attempt to persuade their respective duellists to change their minds, but neither would back down and when the pistols had been loaded, the ground measured, and the Duke of Winchilsea in position, only fate could take a hand in what might turn out be a historical tragedy.

Wellington raised his pistol, aimed at Winchilsea's chest, moved his aim well to the left and fired.

Winchilsea then raised his pistol, aimed it above his head and fired into the air.

The Duke duelling with Lord Winchilsea on Battersea Fields in 1829, from a contemporary cartoon

Life having been preserved and honour seeming to have been done, Lord Falmouth presented the Duke with a letter written by Winchilsea admitting wrong.

The Duke scanned it and handed it back.

'This won't do,' he said. 'It is no apology. "Regrets" is no apology.'

Winchilsea agreed to alter his 'regrets' to an 'apology' which Wellington then accepted.

The duel was over.

Scolded on his return for breakfast at Number 10 by Harriet Arbuthnot, Wellington explained, 'It was necessary. It was not a private quarrel, but an act of public policy. It went to the heart of my programme and my standing as Prime Minister.'

'It was rash,' Harriet argued, 'especially in a man who will soon have three more children to look after.'

Wellington's solicitor had called to convey that Long-Wellesley had lost his appeal against his guardianship of the children and the way was now open for the Duke to make the situation permanent.

After which matters got better. The Emancipation Bill was passed with a thumping majority in both Commons and Lords, and the Duke's new children enjoyed the spring in Hampshire with Kitty.

Wellington's friends congratulated him on turning Great Britain from the slaughterhouse it could have been to the lake of tranquillity it now was, and it was generally believed, among his own set anyway, that the duel had turned the tide. Once a politician puts his life where his policy is, it has the most powerful effect on public opinion. It was also reported that His Majesty so admired Wellington that he was telling people he wished he had fought the duel himself.

'It's only a matter of time before he believes he did!' commented the Duke.

Despite his change of direction on Catholic Emancipation, Wellington stood quite firm in his beliefs that extending the vote to the majority would lead to anarchy and that only the ruling classes were intelligent enough to take important decisions regarding affairs of State. Though opposition grew stronger he did not budge. 'As far as I am concerned, while I hold any station in government,' he declared, 'I shall always feel it my duty to resist any such measures.'

His popularity dropped.

He was jeered by the mobs, who went so far as throwing bricks through the windows of Number 10 in protest, but he trusted that his real enemies, the Whigs, the Radicals and the Canningites, would be too divided to combine against him.

On 15 November 1830 the Government was defeated in the House, Wellington resigned and was succeeded by the Whig, Lord Grey. The Duke now did not want to go into Opposition.

They want me to place myself at the head of a faction; but I say to them, I have now served my country for forty years – for twenty I have commanded her armies, and for ten I have sat in the Cabinet – and I will not now place myself at the head of a faction. When I lay down my office tomorrow, I will go down into my county and do what I can to restore order and peace. And in my place in Parliament, when I can, I will approve; when I cannot I will dissent; but I will never agree to be the leader of a faction.

Not long after, however, he was persuaded to lead the Opposition and he immediately regretted it. For, if he had learned that a Prime Minister's authority was considerably less than that of a general, he now discovered that an Opposition leader had no authority at all. 'Nobody does anything but what he likes, excepting myself. We are all commanders, and there are no troops. Nobody obeys or ever listens to advice but myself. Then I am

An anonymous aquatint of the Duke of Wellington

abused because things do not go right.'

He had a simple strategy – to go on rejecting the Reform Bill in order to gain time, and he urged his Tories to close ranks. He was labelled an 'ultra', a fashionable term of the time for an extreme reactionary. In April the Whigs were defeated in the House of Lords, but the Duke was unfortunately not there to see victory. Kitty was dying at Apsley House, and he was by her side.

With the dissolution of Parliament a riotous mob was moving through the streets of London looking for dark windows: sure signs of Tory residences trying to keep a low profile. Apsley House, in mourning, was very dark, so the crowd started to throw stones, breaking the glass, until an outraged servant blasted a blunderbuss over their heads. The next day the Duke installed iron shutters to protect his windows, which caused a further fall in his popularity. He was hanged in effigy in the slum area of Seven Dials, an incident which did not particularly offend him.

Reform was inevitable. George IV had been succeeded in 1830 by his brother William. Now, two years later, William IV was facing the possibility of having to create Whig peers to please his Government. Determined to avoid such a disastrous move, Wellington withdrew his opposition to the bill. His supporters returned to their country houses and clubs while the bill passed through its final stages, and in the summer of 1832 the royal assent was read out to a House of Lords packed with Whigs but empty of Tories.

In 1834 Melbourne, who had followed Grey as Prime Minister, was dismissed and Wellington was summoned by the King to act as Prime Minister for three weeks, until Sir Robert Peel should return from a visit to Italy. During this time he was First Lord of the Treasury, Home Secretary, Foreign Secretary, and Minister of War.

'His Highness the Dictator is concentrating in himself all the powers of the State,' declared Grey, while another Whig claimed that if the choice was between such despotism and anarchy, he would prefer anarchy.

Although burdened with an overload of work, the Duke coped admirably. Essential policy decisions were perhaps delayed while he dealt with administrative details, but he was glad to be kept busy, for his dear friend Harriet Arbuthnot had just died of cholera, a private grief on which he did not wish to dwell.

When Peel returned to London Wellington gave up all his offices, except that of Foreign Secretary, and when in 1835 Peel was succeeded by Melbourne, the Duke went out of office.

He was eventually to recapture his popularity. He was installed as Chancellor of Oxford University, made Warden of the Cinque Ports, and in 1841 Queen Victoria asked him to form yet another Government when Melbourne was defeated. He declined her invitation in favour of Peel, but accepted the post of Foreign Secretary and became Leader of the House of Lords until Peel resigned five years later.

He hoped to find peace when he retired to Walmer Castle, the official residence of the Warden of the Cinque Ports. To his horror he found he was plagued by an unexpected army of artists and portrait painters, bent on depicting him. He had 'no objection to any gentleman painting any picture of me that he may think proper; but if I am to have anything to say to the picture, either in way of sitting or sending a dress, I consider myself, and shall be considered by others, as responsible for it. To paint the Emperor Napoleon on the rock of St Helena is quite a different thing from painting me on the field of the battle of Waterloo.'

The death-bed scene of the Duke of Wellington at Walmer Castle, 14 September 1852. An engraving by John Gilbert

On 14 September 1852, in Walmer Castle, he got up as usual, went to sit at his desk and ordered his carriage for a drive to Dover. A while later he told his manservant, 'I feel very ill, send for the apothecary.'

These were his last words. He died shortly afterwards sitting in the high-backed chair.

He was eighty-three.

CHAPTER FOUR

Old Glad Eyes

Sex ceased to be talked about openly in the latter half of the nineteenth century. It was considered better to be preoccupied by sex than occupied by it, and there is no better example of a man who practised this doubtful Victorian compromise than William Ewart Gladstone. When he was Prime Minister, he openly invited prostitutes to Number 10 Downing Street, though he was, to all appearances, fervently religious.

The fourth son of Sir John Gladstone, a successful Liverpool merchant, William was born in 1809 and educated at Eton and Christ Church, Oxford, where he gained a double first in classics and mathematics. Though he entered Lincoln's Inn, he thought himself destined for the Church and wanted to take Holy Orders, but was dissuaded from this by his family who convinced him that he could be of just as much service to mankind by going into politics. He followed their advice and at the age of twenty-three he was returned as Tory Member of Parliament for Newark in Nottinghamshire.

In 1833 he made his maiden speech during a debate on the abolition of slavery in the British Empire. His father owned slaves on a sugar plantation in Demerara and Gladstone, apparently genuine in the belief that it would not be in the interest of slaves for them to be set free, opposed their emancipation. His oratory brought him to the notice of the Prime Minister, Sir Robert Peel, who appointed him Junior Lord of the Treasury and then Under-Secretary at the Colonial Office. When Peel resigned a few months later, Gladstone went with him into opposition for the next six years. During this period he wrote a book entitled *The State in its Relation to the Church*, which won him the label of 'The rising hope of the stern unbending Tories'.

In 1839 he married the elder daughter of an aristocratic, rich, land-owning Whig family, Catherine Glynne, a tall, slender, wide-eyed girl whom he had first met in a German resort where she had gone to recover from being jilted by an eligible suitor, and where he was recovering from overwork and grief over his mother's death.

William Ewart Gladstone as a rising young Tory politician

Catherine's background was that of a typical upper-class young lady, not too highly educated but fluent in French and Italian, fond of reciting poetry at great length, and capable of running the not insignificant family seat – Hawarden Castle in Flintshire – as her mother had become an invalid. But while William Gladstone was methodical, ordered, and spent hours sitting in one place reading, Catherine Glynne was untidy, restless and constantly on the go.

They moved into their first London home at Number 11 Carlton House Terrace, immediately setting up a library below stairs for the specific use of the servants, and establishing morning breakfasts at 10.00 a.m. by way of entertaining anyone who wanted to visit them. William Ewart Gladstone was always at his best in the mornings.

In 1841 Peel again became Prime Minister and appointed Gladstone Vice-President of the Board of Trade, then President. The country was in economic trouble; unemployment was high and trade was poor, but with various reforms Peel succeeded in getting things on a more even keel.

In 1844 he turned his attention to Ireland and, believing that a better training for the clergy would lead to better government in that country, he proposed to increase a State grant to the Catholic college at Maynooth. Though this could be termed a minor Church matter, Gladstone, who had upheld the view that the State could only promote one religious faith in his book, *The State in its Relation to the Church,* felt obliged to resign. He was thus out of office when the debates began concerning the repeal of the Corn Laws.

The Corn Laws had been brought in during the war against France in 1815, banning the importation of foreign corn in order to keep the price of British corn high. Though Peel thought that the laws should be repealed, the majority of the Tory Party did not agree, and he could not oppose them. The debates continued for five months, by which time Gladstone rejoined Peel's administration as Colonial Secretary.

The Irish potato crop was then struck by a blight causing starvation and death on a horrific scale. Faced with such a disastrous famine, Peel decided to send wheat to Ireland and, to do so, insisted that the Corn Laws must be repealed.

For some time Gladstone had held the view that there must be some relaxation in the laws, so backed his leader. But Benjamin Disraeli, who at forty-two had so far been rejected by Peel for a Cabinet post, sought revenge for the slight by heading an influential group demanding the retention of the Corn Laws.

Gladstone, not understanding the burning spirit inside ambitious men who had to struggle against the currents of class and religious prejudice, could only see Disraeli's attacks on their leader as disloyal and vicious, and from then on had a deep distrust of Disraeli's actions and motives.

After carrying the repeal of the Corn Laws, Peel's Government was

The Glynne sisters: left, Catherine, who married William Gladstone; right, Mary, who became Lady Lyttelton. From a drawing by J. Slater

resoundingly defeated, the Tory Party was split into two and Gladstone was left without a seat in the Cabinet or in the Commons. Following Peel as a liberal conservative, Gladstone returned a year later as Member of Parliament for Oxford University. He joined a group of unhappy displaced persons who voted sometimes with the Whigs, sometimes with former colleagues. Disraeli rarely lost a chance to remind him of his desertion of the Tory Party.

In 1852 the Earl of Derby became Prime Minister and Disraeli was appointed Chancellor of the Exchequer. A general election caused a stalemate between Whigs and Tories, the Peelites holding the balance. When Disraeli produced a disastrous budget, Gladstone in a brilliant speech that was to establish him as one of the great orators, described it as 'fraudulent chimaeras of enchanters and magicians'. As a result it was rejected by the House, bringing about the eventual downfall of the Government. The speech was to be the first of many verbal duels between Gladstone and Disraeli, the former's invariably dull and verbose but moral, the latter's cutting, witty and vitriolic.

While Gladstone thus gained recognition as a superior master of parliamentary debate, at home Catherine produced no less than eight children, while coping with her own family problems.

Her brother, having inherited Hawarden, proved incapable of running it properly and the estate went bankrupt. But with William's help and her own thriftiness, Catherine saved it and the Castle became their country house. She immediately opened the park to the public, wanting everyone to enjoy it. She also gave unemployed men work on the estate and sheltered needy children from the Lancashire cotton famine, at times providing over one thousand meals a day.

Catherine was known for her strange use of the English language. The Glynnes, like many families, had over the years developed their own slang and are said to have originated such phrases as 'to die of laughter' and to be 'over the moon'. She never stopped inventing: 'the issue is vull,' she would say, meaning it was null and void; or 'his life is lived on a pinnacle' about William; or 'he really is A2' about someone she found disappointing. Staying at Hawarden while her husband was in London, she wrote him confusing letters, mixing up domestic problems with politics and local gossip, all of which he was apparently able to decipher.

She was not, perhaps, the ideal wife for a statesman, showing little tolerance towards the people that she found boring. She never went out of her way to invite the right guests to dinner, or to behave diplomatically to those who might be of use to William in furthering whatever cause he was pursuing. But in many ways this was not important: William and Catherine were blessed with an enduring relationship with common interests that overcame any disagreements. Together they formed a partnership which seemed to fulfil Victorian demands for perfect matrimony.

Nor was there anything prim about them. Many a night they would roll up to bed, arms around each other's waists, singing raucous music hall catches. Catherine's weird private slang, sense of fun and incorrigible untidiness delighted Gladstone.Their easy affection for each other is perhaps best summarized by the song they would sing together, at the least excuse, in front of the fire: 'A ragamuffin husband and a rantipoling wife, we'll fiddle it and scrape it through the ups and downs of life'.

In 1853 Gladstone followed Disraeli as Chancellor of the Exchequer in Lord Aberdeen's coalition ministry and had to consider whether he wanted to live at Number 11 Downing Street. He went to look at the house and reported to Catherine that he was 'agreeably surprised with its goodness both as to accommodation and state'.

The Gladstone family happily moved in as Disraeli moved out, but a prolonged row developed over the rightful ownership of the furniture and Chancellor's robes, resulting in an acrimonious exchange of letters between the two men.

Gladstone proved to be a brilliant financier and his first budget was a notable success, reducing income tax, which he would have abolished altogether had it not been for the Crimean War. He continued as Chancellor under Lord Palmerston until 1859, then under Lord John Russell until 1866. He became leader of the Liberal Party a year later and Prime Minister on winning the election of 1868.

During this time his private life was equally active, but not always fortunate. One of his daughters, Jessy, died of meningitis; then his sister-in-law Mary died, leaving twelve children, which Catherine decided to adopt. This meant that when Gladstone went to Hawarden for a rest he now found a household with no less than nineteen infants and adolescents and as many adults, including the servants.

When William became Prime Minister the Gladstones did not move to Number 10 but returned to Carlton House Terrace. It was not until 1880, twelve years later, after Disraeli had again come to power and again been defeated, that Gladstone moved to Downing Street. Thereafter it became the settled practice for the First Lord of the Treasury – with the exception of Lord Rosebery for one year – to reside at the famous address.

In 1880 Gladstone was seventy-one. He was to hold office for five years, lose it for six months, regain it for six months, lose it once more, and become Prime Minister again for the fourth time. It was during this second term of office, when he had just made Downing Street his home, that he sailed so close to the wind of scandal that members of his Cabinet feared he would scuttle himself and the whole party.

Since the time of his daughter, Jessy's, death, he had started to increase his activities working among the London prostitutes. Both he and Catherine

'The people's William', a cartoon by Spy, 1879

were members of the Church Penitentiary Association for the Reclamation of Fallen Women. They had founded the Clewer House of Mercy near Oxford, the Newport House of Refuge in Soho Square and St Mary Magdalen House of Refuge in Paddington. Catherine, following the opening of such a refuge, wrote, 'Yesterday I took a poor young thing to the new house, picked her up in Windmill Street and left her safe.' Presumably Gladstone, too, used to visit the girls in such an establishment to talk to them or to bring a new waif, hoping that after a short stay she would go back into society refreshed and rehabilitated. But it is likely that, shielded from the real world as he was by his eminent position, he could not know the girls' true needs, however much he thought he understood them by frequenting their company.

That prostitution in Victorian England was rife among the working classes was due above all to financial desperation. It was accepted by many husbands that their wives might walk the streets to supplement their scant earnings and to keep the family from starvation. It was not unknown for a man to hire his wife out for a pint of beer, and in Nottingham it was recorded that a man sold his wife for a penny. The price included the length of rope tied round her neck.

In the West End of London, however, prostitution was a lucrative and secure business; the police rarely interfered and the only intrusion was by do-gooders and clergymen who did not want to understand or admit that the girls might actually enjoy their trade, and did not feel it was degrading or sordid. Victorian morality wished an attitude on to prostitutes, needing to see them as sinners longing for repentance.

Early in Victoria's reign, when social convention was less strait-laced, matters dealing with sex could be discussed, but once Victoria and Albert had imposed their moral code, the whole subject became taboo. Concern over venereal disease, however, caused the 'Great Social Evil' to be debated in the House when it became necessary to pass the Contagious Diseases Acts. This series of measures, introduced between 1864 and 1869, covered such areas as Aldershot, Chatham, Devonport, Plymouth, Windsor, Cork and Queenstown, in an attempt to control the spread of VD in the army and the navy by limiting prostitution. In the heated debates that ensued Gladstone spoke up, knowing, from more experience in the field than others, how complicated implementation of the acts would be: 'I would rather extend than restrict the operation of these acts, but I admit that there is considerable difficulty in defending a system which can only be partially applied as these acts have been.'

Contemporary statistics on prostitution attempted to classify the types of girls engaged on the streets into various categories, but they did not get very far. There were the REGULARS and the IRREGULARS and these were split up under the headings 'Could not write', 'Could write well', 'Educated', and so on. There were the DOLLYMOPS, amateurs, like nannies who picked up

Prostitutes slipping 'sometimes a sovereign, and sometimes less' to the beadle on duty in fashionable Burlington Arcade, Piccadilly

soldiers in the park, and child prostitutes who were the main pleasure of richer men. The latter were helped in satisfying their vices by the extraordinary fact that though puberty was occurring at a later age in Britain than it is today, the age of consent was actually *twelve*.

In 1871, under Gladstone, a Royal Commission was instructed to look into the question, and came up with this report:

The traffic in children for infamous purposes is notoriously considerable in London and other large towns. We think that a child of twelve can hardly be deemed capable of giving consent, and should not have the power of yielding up her person. We therefore recommend the absolute protection of female children to the age of fourteen years, making the age of consent to commence at fourteen instead of twelve as under the existing law.

Gladstone's 'night walks' had become notorious, causing much specu-

William Ewart Gladstone (Denis Quilley), having just been challenged about his night walks by Lord Rosebery

Gladstone (Denis Quilley) with two ladies of the streets, Bessie (Leanne Robinson) and Annie (Jennifer Guy)

William and Catherine Gladstone (Denis Quilley and Celia Johnson) praying together in the hall of Number 10 after hearing of Lord Frederick Cavendish's assassination in Phoenix Park, Dublin

lation. He would leave Downing Street late at night and walk to Soho, where he would engage prostitutes in conversation. He was so well known among the girls that new ones on the beat were warned by the old hands not to get involved with him. Whether or not he cared to admit it, it is clear that the mere courting of the girls and the suggestions that he made were sources of gratification. To charm a young street girl with the allurement, 'You won't be sorry my little songbird, I do assure you, this evening could prove to be a turning point in your life,' probably amused him, and when a hardened trouper joined in adding, 'You'll regret it, I've had some, don't say you haven't been warned!' this could but side-track the girl from realizing that he was referring to a sermon which would aim to purify her.

Often he would bring the girls to Downing Street, usually taking them straight to the kitchen, where they would be fed by the staff, who were used to their master's habits, after which he would take them upstairs to the drawing room and attempt to convert them.

On one such night, shortly after the cook's niece had arrived fresh from the country to start work as a skivvy, Gladstone brought for a meal two ladies, brazenly overdressed to flaunt their wares. The innocent skivvy, having been told that she was working for the most important man in the country, was terrified when he came in with the girls. 'They be harlots!' she screamed, 'I'm in one of them brothels, that's where I am. I've been captured into a brothel. I'm fetching the police.' Which she might well have done if Catherine had not come down at that moment on hearing the uproar, and calmed her down. 'It is the duty of us all in this life,' she explained to the nervous skivvy, 'to help those less fortunate than ourselves. That is what Mr Gladstone does, tries to do, and I do my best to help him.'

It was not uncommon for members of the Cabinet, calling late at Number 10 on some important issue, to find the drawing room still filled with cheap scent, or even to pass a prostitute in the hallway as she was being shown out by the butler. Lord Granville, the Foreign Secretary, for example, was kept waiting one evening while Gladstone, who had failed to convince two ladies that they could lead a more pious life, got down on his knees to pray out loud, 'Lord, forgive me my failure with two forlorn creatures this evening. And give me strength to continue my efforts.' Granville was then shown in to announce that a telegram had just been received from Dublin concerning further riots in Armagh.

Gladstone was a believer in the right of small nations to govern themselves, and when the Liberals won the election in 1880, he had made it clear that his intention was to pacify Ireland. As many opposed him it was suggested that he should have a permanent bodyguard against attack from fanatics. He turned down the idea point blank, creating further concern, for no one was quite sure whether he was protecting his dubious night walks or truly needed a sense of freedom.

William and Catherine Gladstone surrounded by their family at Hawarden

He certainly believed in talking directly to the public: he had won his second election by an unprecedented personal tour of Scotland, accompanied only by Catherine, and considered informality with the crowds to be essential. When it was pointed out that he was now living in turbulent times with anarchists and revolutionaries throwing bombs indiscriminately, he replied, 'Explosions are the drums behind the symphony of British history. We are singularly insensitive to loud noises.'

When Sir William Harcourt, the Home Secretary, went nearer the bone, warning him of the dangers of footpads, sandbaggers, muggers, and women who could knot a scarf round his neck and strip him of his possessions without his being able to make a sound or defend himself, and adding that his nocturnal perambulations made him a particular target, he simply replied that he had been engaged in night walks for thirty-five years and he had never yet met a woman who had shown him anything but courtesy.

Home life at Downing Street went on as usual, the vast family revolving round Catherine's luncheons and tea parties. Grandchildren, grandnephews and grandnieces were always free to rush in on the Prime Minister, even though he might be working out how best to solve an international problem, affectionately calling him 'Bill', then being scolded

107

Lord Frederick Cavendish, who was married to Catherine's favourite niece, Lucy. He was sent to Ireland as Chief Secretary by Gladstone, and was brutally murdered in Phoenix Park, Dublin

for doing so by one of their more respectful nannies. A frequent visitor to the house was Lucy, Catherine's favourite niece – the daughter of her late sister Mary. She had married Lord Frederick Cavendish whom Gladstone appointed Chief Secretary for Ireland in 1880.

On the night after this young man's departure to Ireland, Catherine returned alone from a dinner she had attended with Gladstone at the Austrian embassy to learn that Cavendish had been brutally murdered in Phoenix Park, Dublin. Following the dinner she had gone on alone to a party at the Admiralty, expecting William to have already come home, but he had gone off on one of his night walks and no one knew where he was.

Fortunately he did not roam the streets for too long on this occasion and, on returning and hearing of the tragedy, instantly dropped to his knees in the front hall to pray, 'Oh Lord, look on with mercy and take into thy love thy good servant Frederick Cavendish who died this day in the service of his country and shine on him thy eternal light, which washes away all sin and admit him into bliss everlasting. Amen.'

When Lucy Cavendish arrived shortly afterwards to have the fearful news confirmed, she was so shaken at seeing how distraught her uncle was that she begged him not to blame himself for having sent her husband on the Dublin mission.

Cavendish's assassination proved to be more than a personal blow to Gladstone. Added to his grief came more pressure for him to accept personal police surveillance, which he was loath to authorize. But it had become necessary and from now on, wherever he went, a plain clothes man was close behind, watching his every move.

It did not take him long to turn this setback into a game, and it became evident to police officers that to be assigned the honour of being the Prime Minister's bodyguard was in no way a sinecure. Gladstone played cat and mouse with his detectives, giving them the slip whenever he could, and accepting their expertise amiably when they caught up with him. But one night, when Fenian bombs were bursting around the capital, he chose to lose them altogether.

By 2.00 a.m. he had not returned to Downing Street and his disappearance was treated as a major emergency. Police searched high and low, but could find no trace of him. In one brothel the Madame crossed her heart and swore, 'I'll take my oath, Old Glad Eyes ain't been here tonight. And glad I am of it. He only unsettles the girls. He's either a knave or a saint, and I'm blessed if I know which. But God has a way of looking after both species.'

In the drawing room of Number 10, Lord Granville, the Foreign Secretary, Sir Edward Hamilton, Gladstone's personal Secretary, and Sir William Harcourt, the Home Secretary, paced the floor nervously considering what fate could have befallen their Prime Minister and how they would deal with the crisis. Added to their worries was concern over what to tell Mrs

A bomb attack by Fenians on government offices in Whitehall, 1883

Gladstone and how she would react when she learned that the police were looking for her husband. However, when Harcourt explained the situation to her, she was neither surprised nor distressed. 'If I quote her accurately,' he told the others, 'she murmured something about it being very gaunt of him and he must have the Housums.' Translated into normal English this meant that she thought it rather irritating of him, but that he must have political worries.

Lord Rosebery, Secretary for Foreign Affairs and later to succeed Gladstone as Prime Minister, then joined them and urged that, when he returned, one of them should speak to the Premier. It was all very well going out every night with the intention of reforming fallen women, but his missions weren't showing any outward signs of success. In three years he had apparently only managed to reclaim ten or so persons to his complete satisfaction, and one of those was a young woman whom he described as being 'at the top of the tree', a pretty young thing who had been married at fifteen and had been on the game ever since, working from an apartment in Brompton Square and keeping a carriage and pair. When Gladstone had declared to all that she was reformed, he was promptly saddled with a bill from the proprietor of some stables in fashionable Cheval Place, who wrote to him, 'I feel justified in asking you to pay the heavy account.' The girl, who had lost her earning power, obviously couldn't.

The women that Gladstone chose to help were usually pretty and invariably worked in the less unpleasant parts of London, which led his critics to have genuine doubts as to his real motives.

A parliamentary colleague, Henry Labouchere, publicly voiced that 'Gladstone manages to combine his missionary meddling with a keen appreciation of a pretty face. He has never been known to rescue any of our East End whores, nor for that matter is it easy to contemplate his rescuing any ugly woman, and I am quite sure his conception of Magdalen is of an incomparable example of pulchritude with a superb figure and carriage.'

Coventry Patmore, sharp-tongued poet of Biblical eroticism, also wrote disparagingly, 'His leprosy's so perfect, men call him clean!'

One lady whom he tried to convert was known as Sweet Nelly Fowler, and was famous enough to be written about in a book entitled *London in the Sixties* by D. Shaw: 'This beautiful girl had a natural perfume so delicate, so universally admitted, that love sick swains paid large sums of money for the privilege of having their handkerchiefs placed under the Goddess's pillow, and Sweet Nelly pervaded – in spirit, if not the flesh – half the clubs and drawing rooms of London.'

And Sweet Nelly Fowler herself wrote of Gladstone: 'The Prime Minister actually called to see me. He is not at all as stern as they all say he is, but most well mannered, kind and considerate, and, indeed, a wonderful figure of a man, so very, very handsome, that one longs to stroke that magnificent head.'

Lord Rosebery, Gladstone's Secretary for Foreign Affairs. He drew the short straw when it was decided that Gladstone must be tackled about his notorious night walks, but found his Prime Minister a formidable opponent

In answer to allegations that he was hitting his head against a succulent but obdurate wall in trying to convert the unconvertible, Gladstone admitted that the task he had chosen to take on was no easy one. 'I know from personal experience, ' he claimed, 'that these women dread, yes, actually dread going back into the kind of ordered, decent world they have left behind.' All of which made his Liberal colleagues extremely sensitive as to what the Party's enemies might dig up.

One aspect of the situation in his favour was that he had always been totally open about what he was doing. Three quarters of a miserably paid and highly bribable police force witnessed his activities, yet no one had so far bought a scandal from them. He and Catherine had set up their institutions, and were helped by Lady Frederick Cavendish and other high-minded ladies of impeccable reputation. On the other hand, these worthy ladies did not actively seek out prostitutes in their haunts, nor find it necessary to enter brothels and to disappear for hours at a time at night.

On the night of his disappearance, when he was still missing at 3.00 a.m., the assembled ministers decided to ask Gladstone's son, Stephen, who was Rector of Hawarden, to speak to him when he returned. Stephen was staying at Downing Street and seemed to be the ideal person, but he refused on the grounds that if he spoke to his father it would lend family credence to the gossip and it was too delicate a matter.

Credence, it was pointed out to him, had already been lent in a more important quarter than the family. Her Majesty Queen Victoria's dislike of Gladstone had partly stemmed from the gossip that *she* had heard, however inaccurate.

'My father is the purest, simplest, most innocent Christian I know,' Stephen countered, adding that he believed the only reason his father had gone into politics was to put Christian principles into practice in daily life. The staunchness and clarity he instilled in all his family had persuaded his son to take the cloth. To discuss such matters would be tantamount to an accusation, and he could not do that.

The issue was so critical, however, that Rosebery and Hamilton decided Gladstone had to be tackled. They tossed a coin to see which of them would take the bull by the horns.

Rosebery lost.

Gladstone did not return home that night, but appeared at breakfast time cheerful and delighted at seeing members of his Cabinet up so early. He instantly engaged them all in a morning prayer, making him seem so innocent and pure that no one dared bring up the subject. Instead, they discussed the invasion of Afghanistan by the Russians and news by telegraph from Egypt that Arabi Pasha had attacked Alexandria, resulting in the murder of a number of foreigners – all of which the Prime Minister announced he would deal with at a meeting within the hour, before sweeping out of the room.

But for the arrival at that moment of an envelope addressed to Lord Rosebery, it is possible that no one would have had the courage to talk to the Prime Minister. However, when the unexpected letter was brought in by the butler and Rosebery scanned it, he realized that he had something to help him confront the Premier.

Gladstone, in the study, was on his knees praying when Rosebery came in. The young man told him he had drawn the short straw and had to talk to him. The Prime Minister thereupon remarked how surprised he was that he was so terrible to talk to that a man had to lose a lottery to do so.

But he proved to be terrible.

When Rosebery suggested that he was endangering the Party, he countered defiantly that he *was* the Party, that he had won the election over the heads of 'parties', that the skies had been crimson with the glow of people's torches on his night of victory, and that the air had quivered with the thunder of their acclaim.

Of what was he being accused?

Rosebery stood his ground, none too tactfully dived in head first, and suggested to the Prime Minister that if he had slept at all during the night it hadn't been in his own bed, that though it wasn't any of their business his ministers were concerned about the night walks, that it was a known fact

Stephen Gladstone, William's clerical son to whom he turned to unburden his guilt

that he had given Lillie Langtry – the actress – the special envelope code so that she could write to him without any of his private secretaries seeing the contents of her letters, that Laura Bell, the rich and fashionable whore, bandied his name about as familiarly as that of her pet spaniel, and finally that on the night of Lord Frederick Cavendish's slaughter in Dublin he had chosen to go off with a young prostitute near the Duke of York Steps, observed by the master of the Bermondsey Workhouse from whom he had just received a letter ending: 'For years that Statesman has been my idol. So much for human frailty and credibility. I almost disbelieved my own eyes and knowledge.'

The realization that he had caused so much anxiety among his admirers and supporters shook Gladstone enough to make him seek help from his son Stephen. It was not because they were related that he turned to him, but because he was a man of the Church and conveniently available. Though what was said between them can only be surmised, it became clear that the Prime Minister's unburdening of guilt added up to a confession, not of evil deeds but of a fearful and – for him – ambiguous commitment which had dogged his life since his student days, and of which Catherine was fully aware.

Aged nineteen and at Oxford, getting his double first, he was a member of a certain private club comprised of earnest young men. Each took an oath that when he had come into his fortune he would devote one tenth of it every year to a charitable cause. They had drawn lots to see which cause would be taken by whom and Gladstone had drawn Fallen Women, an unhappy stroke of fate in his case, for he was already trying to suppress a phenomenal excess of sexual energy.

He was innocent in sexual matters, and considered that his safety valve was his extraordinary political dynamism and stamina. In earlier days he had resorted to self-flagellation to control his urges, apparently being familiar with this form of masochism. He revealed himself as an enthusiast of systematic flogging. In later years his prodigious felling of trees was thought to be another form of sublimation. He was still creating havoc in his forests in his seventies.

Gladstone's headmaster at Eton had been Dr John Keate, a notorious figure in the flogging history of that school. At an old boys' dinner in 1841, which both Keate and Gladstone attended, Keate's popularity with his students became apparent.

In those days at public dinner [Gladstone wrote], cheering was mounted in graduations. I suppose it to be beyond doubt that of the assembled company the vastly predominating majority had been under his [Keate's] sway at Eton. It is equally beyond doubt that to the persons of the whole of them, with the rarest exceptions, it had been the case of Dr Keate to administer the salutary correction of the birch. But upon this occasion, when his name had been announced, the scene was indes-

CURREY.   PHOTO

*Gladstone was celebrated for his delight in cutting down trees, a pastime that he
continued into old age*

Flagellation, the horrific ritual of Victorian public schools

cribable. The roar of cheering had a beginning, but never knew satiety or end. Like the huge waves of Biarritz, the floods of cheering continually recommenced; the whole process was such that we seemed all to have lost our self-possession and to be hardly able to keep our seats.

The Rev. Stephen Gladstone was dubious about what amounted to receiving a confession from his own father, but that was what the old man wanted. There was a time, Gladstone explained, when he believed that the healthy soul was able to discharge its burdens at the foot of the great throne without the assistance of an intermediary. But he no longer believed that. Though he had championed the rights of small nations, set people free in England, had doubled the number of people entitled to vote and liberated them from penal taxes, he had never been able to liberate himself from the lusts that can manacle a man more surely than irons.

To Stephen's astonishment he declared that he was cursed by an over-abundance of 'that vitality which causes the fruits of the earth and people upon it to increase and multiply'. If he had allowed himself to do so, he claimed, he would have sired eighty families, eight hundred families! He was vulnerable to women; their very sight, their touch, their scent, their conversation even, would spark off the uncontrollable demon within him.

To avoid what the Roman Catholics called 'the occasions of sin' he had left rooms, excusing himself, and had just gone from the presence of the female who excited him, aware that on many occasions this must have seemed strange and very rude. He had also stopped frequenting bookshops, fearing the temptation of pornography, for he had become an avid reader, not so much of the obvious dross turned out by East End print shops, but of the classics, Petronius, Boccaccio and the French *Fabliaux*. He had forced himself as a young man to lead a life as close to that of a monk as was possible for a man who is about in the world.

As to the self-flagellation, he admitted to having had to abandon the practice, realizing that pleasure and pain were insidiously related and that it was possible for the latter to occasion the former. He even speculated that the martyrs in the Middle Ages who were burnt at the stake might have derived pleasure from the agony inflicted by the licking flames.

To his own dismay, on looking back over his life, he realized that he had spent more time than was necessary trying to convert one particular girl, Elizabeth Collins. He thought her as lovely as a statue and had indulged in keeping her company for two or three 'turbulent' hours at a time. He had told himself that he was fighting the Devil for her salvation, but he was no longer sure that had been true. He was not sure whether he had deluded himself in the notion of doing good by mixing with these girls or whether he had actually sought through his good works what he considered to be unlawful.

As to whether he had ever done anything which could be regarded as being unfaithful to his wife, he apparently did not consider that he had been guilty of the act which is known as that of 'infidelity to the marriage bed', a phrase which could be interpreted in many ways.

Whatever relief he got from talking to his son Stephen, he acknowledged the fact that he would have to stop his night walks for the sake of the Party and of his political colleagues. After a short period of abstention, however, one of his vulnerable creatures sent him a note, begging for help, which as a Christian he could not ignore. He met her, successfully put her on the right path and thereafter decided that his work among fallen women was not in vain. So he gradually resumed his night walks.

In 1889 the Gladstones celebrated their golden wedding anniversary. Whatever harm the gossip about William's activities might have caused, people chose to forget it on this occasion. Presents poured in from all quarters, including a silver-gilt inkstand from the Prince of Wales.

Five years later, aged eighty-five, Gladstone went to Windsor to hand in his resignation to Queen Victoria. She had never liked him, but on this

William and Catherine Gladstone in an uncharacteristically solemn pose

occasion treated him with exceptional charm, though she pointedly failed to ask him whom he would recommend as a successor, and granted him no recognition despite his great services to his country and mankind.

He left Number 10 on 12 March 1894 to spend the last five years of his life in retirement at Hawarden where, after a successful cataract operation on the left eye and the threat of blindness removed, he devoted his time to his books. He edited two volumes of Bishop Butler's massive works, translated Horace's poetry, compiled 'Gleanings' from his own memoirs, and contributed articles to theological magazines.

With Catherine he went to Cannes several times on holiday but in 1897 the painful symptoms of cancer started making themselves felt in his cheekbone. Deciding that the Northern chill of Hawarden was not helping, they moved south to Bournemouth, but a year later he learnt that the swelling which had now developed on his palate was malignant and that there was no hope of recovery.

119

Hawarden Castle, the Gladstones' country home in Flintshire

Returning to Hawarden he faced the oncoming of a painful death with all the courage and fortitude which his Christian faith commanded. By May 1898 he was enduring intense pain and being heavily drugged. On 19 May at two o'clock in the morning the whole family was called to his bedside. Catherine knelt by him and held his hand as his breathing grew slower and slower until it stopped.

William Ewart Gladstone was buried at Westminster Abbey and among the pall bearers were two future Kings of England – the Prince of Wales and his son Prince George. However disturbing Old Glad Eyes' inner crises had been for the Victorians, all, in the end, was forgiven.

CHAPTER FIVE
Henry and Margot

For thirteen years, from 1894 to 1907, Number 10 Downing Street lost the family-home atmosphere created by the Gladstones, and became the sedate residence of Premiers of the State. The Earl of Rosebery was a widower, the Marquis of Salisbury chose to live elsewhere, Arthur James Balfour was a bachelor, and Sir Henry Campbell-Bannerman, old and ill, died in the house.

Then the Asquiths arrived, nine of them in all, with fourteen servants. Not only did they charge the air with sophisticated humour, argument and laughter, but the garden was turned into a children's playground, and the street outside into what amounted to a hotel forecourt, with a continuous flow of vehicles coming and going, delivering goods or collecting members of High Society after fashionable luncheon and dinner parties.

Herbert Henry Asquith, however, did not come from a background which foretold a stylish ministry. Born in Morley, a small Yorkshire wool town, in 1852, his childhood was dogged by unusual and relentless tragedy. Two of his three sisters died as infants, his older brother William was kicked in the spine during a football game, resulting in stunted growth. His father, aged only thirty-six, died following a cricketing accident when Herbert was eight, while his mother, Emily, spent most of her life lying on a sofa suffering from bronchitis and a weak heart.

The family were looked after by William Willans, Emily's father, a notable civic figure in Huddersfield, who narrowly missed election to Parliament as a Radical Member for the borough.

He settled the unfortunate Asquiths into a house close to his own and first sent the boys to Huddersfield College, then to a small boarding school at Fulneck. But two years later he died and Emily left Yorkshire for ever, moving south to St Leonards-on-Sea in Sussex with her daughter. She sent William and Herbert to an uncle in London, who took care of their educa-

121

Herbert Asquith, the rising yo[ung] barrister. He was making £10,000 a year by the time h[e] left the bar

tion by placing them with a family in Pimlico as paying guests while they attended the City of London College.

Though the school's curriculum had established leanings towards commerce, it offered its pupils a high standard of classical education to which young Herbert took with great enthusiasm. At sixteen his interests were wide, particularly in the area of politics, and he was a frequent visitor to the House of Commons where he spent afternoons listening to the debates of the great parliamentarians of the time.

He was not, however, serious all the time. A typical adolescent, he wrote to a friend about secret visits to the theatre which he found enthralling, a day spent gazing wide-eyed at a fat lady in a fair booth, and the repulsion he felt on encountering the corpses of five murderers hanging outside Newgate Prison for inspection, half an hour after their execution, white caps pulled down over their heads – a sinister sight that stalked his dreams.

In 1869 Herbert Asquith won one of two classical scholarships awarded by Balliol, Oxford, where he spent his days quietly studying and not particularly mixing with other undergraduates. During his second year he was joined by his brother, with whom he shared rooms for economical as well as family reasons. William, less advanced than Herbert, and only five foot tall due to his early accident, needed the initial security of being with someone he knew.

In 1874 Herbert was the only Balliol man to get a First in Greats as well as the Craven Scholarship, he was awarded a prize fellowship of his college, and in his last year, 1875, he became President of the Oxford Union.

That autumn he went out into the world and found himself for the first time among the aristocratic rich, coaching the Earl of Portsmouth's son at two of the family's country houses in Hampshire and Devon. It was an insight into a lifestyle that he could not have otherwise experienced, and enabled him to listen to the conversations and study the behaviour of some of the most important people in the country.

It was now quite clear in his mind that he wanted to go into politics, and as the law was the accepted door to a parliamentary life for young men without position, at the end of 1875 he went to London on being accepted as a pupil by one of the most distinguished nineteenth-century legal minds, Charles Bowen.

Thankful for his Balliol fellowship, which was a small but useful source of income, he spent the next seven years in chambers. For the first five, his professional income was negligible, but despite this he decided to marry in 1877. The young girl was Helen Melland, the daughter of a Manchester doctor, whom he had met at his mother's while still at Oxford and with whom he had corresponded frequently and met as often as possible.

With a few hundred pounds a year from the fellowship, lectures and journalism bringing a little extra, the young couple moved into a house in Hampstead and settled down to a happy placid life, enlivened by the arrival of their first son, Raymond, in 1878 and Herbert Junior three years later.

With a need for additional money, Asquith supplemented his income by marking the Oxford and Cambridge Certificate examination papers, gave lectures to law students and started writing for the *Economist* and *Spectator*.

In 1883 his third son, Arthur, was born, but by then his career prospects had greatly improved. At thirty, with seven years' standing as a barrister, Asquith was beginning to earn a good living entirely from professional work, and casting an eye towards the political scene. He had become friends with a fellow barrister, R. B. Haldane, who in 1885 was elected member of Parliament for East Lothian. This encouraged Asquith to consider his ambitions more seriously and when a year later Haldane urged him to seek nomination from his neighbouring constituency of East Fife, which was looking for a candidate, he launched himself onto the political stage, winning the seat as a Liberal.

As a member of Parliament he settled happily down to the new life, his

Helen Melland, Asquith's first wife whom he married in 1877. She had no ambitions for him as a politician

wife presenting him with a daughter, Violet, the following year and a fourth son, Cyril, in 1890. But in August 1891 tragedy struck unexpectedly. Asquith had taken the family to Lamlash on the Isle of Arran for a Scottish summer holiday and Herbert Junior went down with influenza. Recovery seemed only a question of medication and rest, but two days later Helen caught the illness and for five days treated herself and her son. The fever grew so much worse that the doctor was called, and immediately diagnosed typhoid. It was too late to help. Whereas little Herbert recovered, Helen sank low and died early in September.

Asquith was left emotionally drained and shocked. After the funeral in a local churchyard, he left the Islands and returned with his grief-stricken children to their Hampstead home. To a friend he wrote about Helen:

She cared little for society, shrank from every kind of publicity and self advertise-
ment, hardly knew what ambition meant. She was more wrapped up in her children
than any woman I have ever known. To me she was always perfect, loyal, sympathetic, devoted; not without pride in such successes as I had; but not the least
anxious for me to 'get on', never sanguine or confident, and as a rule inclined to take
a less hopeful view of things. I used sometimes to reproach her with her 'pessimism'.
. . . She was the gentlest and best of companions, a restricting rather than a
stimulating influence, and knowing myself as I do I have often wondered that we
walked so evenly together.

Had Helen lived, it was said by friends of the Asquiths that a social conflict
might eventually have developed, for she was a woman who preferred her
quiet life, while her husband was on the brink of launching himself into
society to reach the ambitious heights on which he had set his sights. Now,
suddenly, he was free to change his whole life's pattern. He did so by moving
from Hampstead to an apartment in Mount Street, Mayfair, and settling the
children in a house in Dorking in Surrey, with a series of housekeepers,
nannies and nursery-maids to look after them.

In 1892 there was a General Election, Gladstone became Prime Minister
for the fourth time and he appointed Asquith Home Secretary. News of this
reached him in the shape of a very simple letter, delivered while he was
dining at his club in St James's.

SECRET.   HAWARDEN CASTLE. CHESTER.
                                                                    Aug. 14.92.

My dear Asquith,
I have the pleasure of writing to propose
that you should allow me to submit your
name to Her Majesty for the office of
Home Secretary.
I have understood that you are willing to
quit your practice at the bar and in consequence
I find myself able to offer this just and I
think signal tribute to your character,
abilities and eloquence.
              Believe me
              Very faithfully yours,

                                                    W. E. GLADSTONE.

A few years before, he had met a vivacious young lady, Margot Tennant,
who was at the time causing a good deal of furore in the more staid circles of
Society. She was the daughter of Charles Tennant, a Scottish businessman,
who was running one of the largest chemical works in the world. The
family's background could best be described as rich upper middle class.
They lived in Glasgow and, until Charles inherited the business, their life

Margot Tennant, the vivacious, eccentric Society girl who became Asquith's second wife to the astonishment and dismay of his more sober colleagues

Laura Tennant, Margot's beloved sister who died in childbirth

was dull and limited. But, aware that riches were not enough to make him totally acceptable in High Society, he built 'Glen', a baronial fantasy in the Peebleshire hills.

They were a large family of brothers and sisters but Margot, born in 1863, lived for Laura her older sister by five years, and Laura lived for her. They were inseparable to the point that they dressed alike and slept together in the nursery in small children's beds when they were well past their early teens, spending their whole time discussing love, life, literature and arguing the nights away, sometimes not getting to sleep till it was time to have breakfast.

Five foot two inches tall, Margot was not as pretty as Laura. In fact she had no illusions about her flat chest and skinny body, nor about her very thin long face. 'I have no face,' she once said, 'only two profiles.' But she had the gift of fascination.

In 1881 both sisters were launched on London Society, behaving outrageously enough for Queen Victoria to disapprove, but amusingly enough for Mrs Gladstone to remark about a visit to Glen, 'I couldn't describe it, it is the maddest, merriest whirl from morn till night, wonderful quickness, brightness, wit, cleverness, the four sisters all so fascinating.'

Margot and Laura were the precursors of the 1920s flappers, Noel Coward characters waiting for him to be born.

Margot as a child was uncontrollable and as an adolescent worse. On one occasion she climbed up on the Glen roof by moonlight, a precipitous and slippery escapade which thrilled her to death and very nearly caused it. On another occasion she rode her pony up the front steps and into the entrance hall which, she had heard, was a traditional ceremony at Sandhurst.

She would set out on her pony early in the morning and spend the entire day roaming the hills and glens, sharing her midday bread and cheese with any shepherd or poacher she might meet.

She was not particularly well educated but read a great deal in her father's library and was quick to pick up facts from other people's conversation. This caused a Balliol professor to comment, 'She is the best educated ill educated woman I have ever met.'

Laura married when she was twenty-three, which left Margot rather alone. But she continued to charm Society with her wit, receiving a flood of invitations after she had spent an afternoon entertaining the Prince of Wales in the Royal Box at Ascot with her unconventional and sometimes irreverent conversation.

In 1887 Laura became pregnant and when the day of the birth drew near, Margot decided she could not stand the tension or bear to see her sister in pain, so disappeared up to Glen and spent her time riding. Urging her horse over a stone wall she fell and, concussed, had to take to her bed.

Falling off horses was not an unusual occurrence for Margot. In the course of her riding life she suffered no less than a broken nose, broken ribs, broken knee caps, both collar bones fractured, a dislocated jaw, a fractured skull and several concussions.

When news came through that Laura had given birth to a boy but was herself severely ill, Margot forgot her own injuries and rushed up to London, only to reach her sister's bedside as Laura was dying.

The tragedy left Margot truly alone, she became highly strung, working off her nervous energy even more on the hunting field. Winston Churchill, a friend of the family, wrote of her, 'Few riders were able to surpass this featherweight daredevil, mounted upon enormous horses, who with faultless nerve and thrust and inexhaustible energy, spurred by love of chase and desire to excel, came sometimes to grief but always to the fore.'

It was in 1891 that she was first introduced to Herbert Asquith, a meeting she described in her autobiography:

I sat next to him in the House of Commons. I had never heard of him, which gives some indication of how much I was wasting my time. . . . I was deeply impressed by his conversation and his clear Cromwellian face. I thought then, as I do now, that he had a way of putting you not only at your ease but at your best when talking to him which is given to few men of note. He was different to the others and, although unfashionably dressed, had so much personality that I made up my mind at once that this was the man who could help me and would understand everything. It never occurred to me that he was married, nor would that have affected me in any way.

The party had gone out on the terrace of the House and Margot and Asquith retired into a shadowed corner, deep in conversation. Their friends left one by one and, not seeing them, assumed they had gone too. When dawn broke over the Thames, Margot and Asquith found themselves alone, having talked the night away. She wrote in her diary that he was the first 'serious' man she had ever met and meeting him made her realize how she had wasted her life until then. 'After this we saw each other constantly.'

Margot met Helen Asquith, whom she found 'gentle and unambitious. She spoke to me of her home and children with love and interest which seemed to exclude her from a life of political aggrandizement. . . . When I said to her she had married a man who was to attain the highest political distinction, she replied that that was not what she coveted for him.'

After his wife's death, Asquith's friends watched Herbert's relationship with Margot develop, first with fascination, not believing it would last, then with alarm as rumour spread that they might actually get married. Lord Rosebery was of the opinion that such a match would ruin Asquith's promising career, while Lord Randolph Churchill could not believe that this 'frivolous magpie-minded creature of society' could be taken seriously as a hard-working politician's wife. Nor was Asquith the first politician with whom her name had been linked. At one point it was rumoured that she was to marry Arthur Balfour. He denied it in typical fashion: 'I rather think of having a career of my own.'

Margot had become so famous as a social butterfly that a novel, supposedly based on her, was published. '*Dodo* by E. F. Benson,' she said, discussing it lightly, was about 'a pretentious donkey with the heart and brain of a linnet.' When the book was left conspicuously in the guest room of a house where he was spending the weekend, Asquith threw it angrily out of the window.

Margot took several years to accept Herbert's eventual proposal of marriage. She was perceptive and honest enough to have doubts about her own capabilities of making such a marriage work. Socially, he was hardly her equal and within her circle he was regarded as a rather donnish eccentric. He hated the modern telephone, for instance, central heating even more, and would never be parted from his quill pen. He had little money, no country house and worst of all no entrée into Society. But one thing which appealed to her was his ready-made family of precocious children who reminded her of her own, slightly lunatic, younger days with Laura.

Physically and temperamentally it was an intriguing match, too. She, thin, hyperactive, a gadfly; he, neolithic, square-cornered, slow-moving. Once urged by Margot to run for a train they were about to miss, he replied mildly. 'I don't run much.'

They married in 1894 when he was forty-one and she was twenty-six. It was a somewhat different wedding from his first, attended at St George's Hanover Square by three Prime Ministers: Gladstone from the past; Lord Rosebery who was then in office; and Balfour who was to become Premier.

She made it known that she would prefer to be called Mrs *Henry* Asquith, rather than Mrs *Herbert*, and from that time Herbert became Henry to his family and friends.

They moved into a roomy rambling house in Cavendish Square, bought for them by Margot's father, and from the moment they had settled she gave innumerable luncheon and dinner parties. The servants had to cope with the fact that the kitchens and their quarters were in a mews behind the main house, and that all the food had to be rushed across an open court-yard. But then there was a small army of servants, fourteen in all, not including the coachman and stable boy.

In 1895 the Government fell, and with no salary, enormous expenses and four sons to educate, Asquith had no option but to return to the Bar, an unusual step for a deposed Cabinet minister. Charles Tennant, who might have been relied on to help, had remarried and Margot had assumed there was no hope of getting anything from Papa. She was proved wrong, however, for Papa came through handsomely, settling £5000 per annum on her for life. This not only took care of the rent on a Scottish house to which the family escaped in the summer, but also paid for her hunting horses. It certainly relieved her husband from the pressure of financial worries.

Illness again haunted Asquith when Margot became pregnant. In May 1895 she was prostrated for three months with phlebitis and lost her first child. Out of five that she carried subsequently, only two were born: Elizabeth in 1897, and Anthony in 1902. After these unpleasant experiences, she suffered continually from insomnia, and when in 1905 the Liberals were swept to power with a massive majority and Henry was appointed Chancellor of the Exchequer under Campbell-Bannerman, she went to St Paul's Cathedral to pray that she might die rather than hamper her husband's life as an invalid.

After another miscarriage, she decided there were to be no more children. When she was asked if she took precautionary measures, her reply was vintage Margot: 'Oh no, Henry always withdraws in time. Such a noble man!'

In 1908 Campbell-Bannerman died at Number 10. On 14 April Asquith was summoned by Edward VII to join him in Biarritz, where he was formally asked to take over the Government. Henry had left London in-

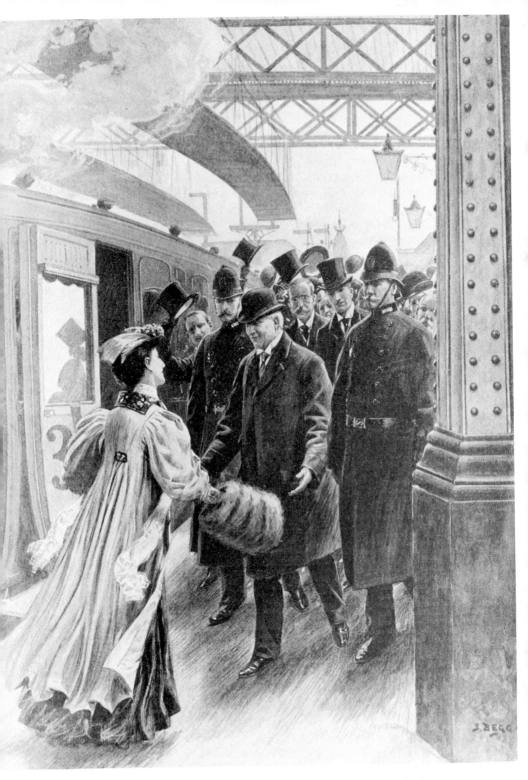

S. Begg's drawing of the scene at Charing Cross Station on 10 April 1908 when Asquith returned from Biarritz as the new Prime Minister to be greeted by the crowds, and Margot

cognito by train, a cap pulled down well over his face, and celebrated the honour of the appointment by announcing it in a typically factual letter to Margot. 'The King said, "I appoint you P.M. and First Lord of the Treasury" whereupon I knelt down and kissed his hand. *Voilà tout!* . . . I leave at 12 noon tomorrow and arrive at Charing Cross 5.12 Friday afternoon. You will no doubt arrange about dinner that evening.'

Margot not only arranged about dinner but waited in the crowd at the station, cheering with excitement at her husband's achievement. She was now the First Lady of the Land after the Queen, and acquaintances in Society who might not have been too kind to her in the past, especially behind her back, would now have to be more circumspect. She also believed that without her social contacts, Henry might not have reached his position so easily, though she never doubted his ability to get there eventually on his own.

Nor was there any doubt about his devotion to her. Normally an undemonstrative man, he once wrote: 'To me, from the first hour I met you until now, you have been the best that I have known. I have loved and love you truly and loyally and with all my nature. God make us ever more to each other and help us both to do and to bear.'

It was early in May 1908 that the Asquith army moved into Number 10 Downing Street. Five-year-old Anthony, known as 'Puffin', his eleven-year-old sister Elizabeth, Violet, about to be launched on her first London Season with all her dresses from Worth; Cyril, her seventeen-year-old brother, as yet undecided about his future; Herbert a writer; Arthur a businessman; and Raymond, at twenty-nine an established barrister. All the servants came along too, and the official Government staff who up to now enjoyed the run of the place found themselves banished to the lower ground floors. They also had very quickly to become accustomed to the fact that affairs of State could be rudely interrupted by any one of the family who thought a personal matter more important. To a five-year-old this could mean the need of support from the Prime Minister in a quarrel with the beastly little girl next door at Number 11: a foreign child from Wales by the name of Megan Lloyd George, who seemed to think that the communicating door between the two houses was hers to open and close at her pleasure. The two children eventually became great friends.

As soon as Asquith was in power he got down to the most pressing business of securing more money to stay ahead in the arms race against Germany, to maintain the old age pension, and to bring in health and unemployment insurance. With Haldane the Home Secretary and Sir Edward Grey, the Foreign Secretary, he discussed the possibility of proposing that anyone with an income of over £5000 a year should pay a land tax. This would be a trifling amount, considering that land increased in value by just being there, but practically everyone in the House of Lords would have to pay the land tax. A finance bill had not been rejected in the Lords for two hundred years, because to do so would be like cancelling the country's bank account, but they recognized that the Lords would not stand for this bill.

In the middle of the discussion on the subject, Margot burst into the Cabinet Room with a problem she was facing on the domestic front. Did Henry know that there was only one bathroom in the whole house, and one bookshelf? 'Has no Prime Minister in history ever washed or read a book?' she asked, incensed.

It was a slight exaggeration as the Cabinet Room was in fact lined with bookshelves.

'They're for Hansard,' she countered. 'Furthermore, the house seems to comprise three grotesque staircases and a tumble of odd little rooms, thrown about through the building like empty potting sheds. I shall have to entertain in the garden!'

'Knowing you, you'll entertain in Horse Guard's Parade if you wish to,' the Prime Minister replied. 'Now if you don't mind . . . policy?'

'Try fitting fourteen servants, two children and five adolescents the size of horses into this hill-billy shack, then talk to me of policy! And incidentally,' she added, 'at this very moment Lord Landsdowne has a parrot cage of peers at Lansdowne House, plotting to bring down your proposed Budget. I just thought you might like to know.'

Margot was ever aware of what else was going on and her network of Society spies seldom failed her when something of importance was brewing, about which her husband could be better informed.

Number 10 started to take on a much livelier aspect than it had ever had before. The Asquiths breakfasted on the long dining room table *en famille* every morning, Henry reading *The Times*, Margot opening her letters, and both trying to ignore the incessant abuse that was hurled across the table by children.

'You going to the Oval today, newt head?'

'Oh God, do I have to put up with you there?'

Violet, now twenty, entering to take her place discreetly, was assailed by further compliments from her younger brothers.

'Wouldn't you think that people who looked like that at breakfast would have the decency to eat in their rooms?'

'Or put a bag over their heads!'

To which she might answer, 'I just saw the cat chewing up one of your end of term essays,' which lie caused an evacuation of the youngest generation while Asquith snorted with laughter at something in his paper: 'If I'd written these speeches for them myself, I couldn't have done them better. Here's a resplendent Marquis declaring that, if the Budget is passed, he'll be compelled to reduce his donation to the London Hospital from five guineas to three! On the opposite page there's a picture of his new yacht –

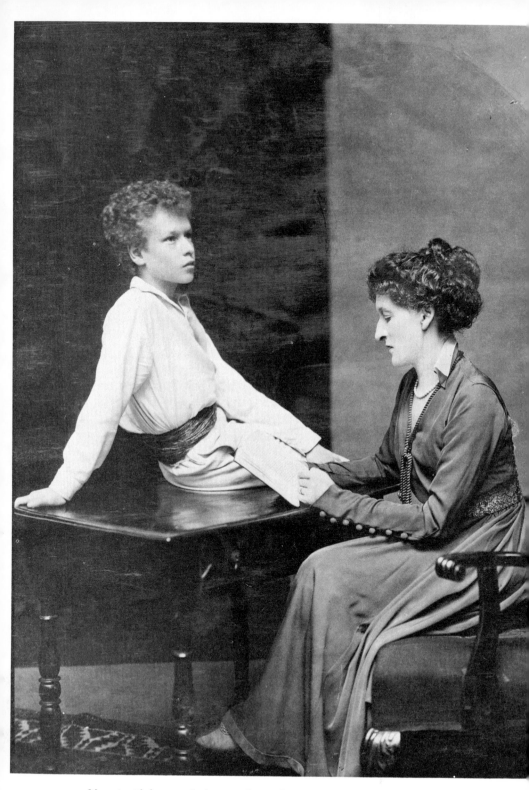

Margot with her son Anthony, nicknamed 'Puffin'. He later became a famous film director

rumoured to have cost him one thousand pounds a month to run!'

'Eleven hundred and fifty,' Margot corrected. 'We're invited on it for August, by the way.'

The whole business of the Budget was becoming so serious that Asquith not only had to talk to the King about it, but talk to him where no one could eavesdrop. They therefore met and walked in Windsor Great Park – Edward VII was curious to know the reason for such precautions.

'A builder of my acquaintance,' explained the Prime Minister, 'once told me the better the brick, the more resounding its acoustic properties. Your Majesty's residences are built of very good bricks indeed.'

'You've the makings of a conspirator,' the King remarked. 'What is it all about?'

Asquith was anticipating a crisis if the aristocracy took the unprecedented step of cutting off the money supply and setting its face against a Budget designed to help the poor, the old and the sick. As head of this aristocracy it would reflect badly on the King. Therefore he must create hundreds of new Liberal peers to swamp the Tory majority in the Lords and push the Budget through.

Edward VII did not think he could do such a thing. It was too drastic a measure and would make a mockery of the system, but, as Asquith pointed out, the system was already absurd. With the Lords against him the Prime Minister could not administer the country and he hinted that perhaps someone else should.

Threatened with Asquith's resignation, which would mean the whole Cabinet going as well, the King suggested that he should hold a general election, making the Budget the prime issue. Then, if Asquith won, the Lords would not dare defy the will of the people.

Asquith protested that if he went to the country and won, he would still have to deal with the blocking power of the Lords. 'I can't hold a general election on every bill they decide to throw out. Will you give me a guarantee, Sir,' he asked, 'that if I win the election, you will create sufficient peers to allow me to get the rest of my legislation through?'

Edward VII did not commit himself, but Asquith did. An election was held in 1910, which he won with a healthy enough majority, though he had to depend on the Irish Unionists and the Labour members to get his measures through. While he struggled with the Lords, Margot struggled with the Ladies to make sure she did not lose her valuable contacts in Society.

Asquith put the Budget through the Commons again, then the Lords. He would not, he said, have 'those bloody landlords to the nation sitting on their upholstered backsides telling him and the House of Commons what they could and what they could not do,' and he intended 'to pluck them from their ancestral boots like snails from their shells, then get on with giving the people of the country a life!'.

Electoral posters for the general election of January 1910. The key issues were Asquith's budget – and the future of the House of Lords

Concerned about future relationships, Margot one day reminded Henry that they spent a good deal of time with the Lords with whom he was threatening to do battle. 'We do go to their dinner parties, we stay at their houses, they add colour and gaiety . . . effervescence to our lives,' she told him. To which he answered, 'Personally, they are delightful. Politically, they are an abomination. I have never had the least difficulty in reconciling the two. And politically they are about to get a fist right between wind and water!'

He planned to prevent the Lords from rejecting or interfering with any measure related to taxation or money by limiting their veto on any bill – to do with money or not – to two years. After such a period a bill could become law whether the Lords liked it or not. The snag was that the very bill that would do all this would itself be vulnerable to the Lords' veto, and they would never pass it.

So again he went to the King, asking him for a tidal wave of new peers. Edward VII again suggested an election, going to the country this time on the issue of a new Parliament Bill. Asquith knew he would have to be patient as well as diplomatic.

Meanwhile, apart from interruptions during Cabinet meetings when

THE CHANCE OF A LIFETIME.

Our Mr. Asquith. "FIVE HUNDRED CORONETS, DIRT-CHEAP! THIS LINE OF GOODS
OUGHT TO MAKE BUSINESS A BIT BRISKER, WHAT?"
Our Mr. Lloyd George. "NOT HALF; BOUND TO GO LIKE HOT CAKES."

*Asquith and Lloyd George preparing to flood the House of Lords with five hundred new
Liberal peers to ensure the passing of the Parliament Bill. From* Punch, *28 December*
1910

Puffin's aeroplane smacked against the windows and his father was obliged to reprimand him, Margot continued to organize Society and her own household. Husband and wife decided they needed a joint social secretary, and one bright morning she interviewed a possible candidate for the job, Maurice Bonham Carter.

It was a typical Margot Asquith encounter.

'Is there anything you'd like to know about me?' she asked the timid young man, who was later to marry Violet.

He replied politely, 'I know you're one of the finest riders to hounds in the country, that you have a gift for music and sketching and that the dancer, Kate Vaughan, seeing you dance, couldn't believe you hadn't been trained for the ballet.'

'All true,' said Margot without too much modesty, 'especially the bits about riding and dancing. I do believe I could have been the first bareback riding circus ballerina in the world. Watch!' Whereupon she started to dance for him but, hampered by her Edwardian dress, she disappeared for a moment from the room to reappear wearing nothing but her combinations.

Humming a theme from *Swan Lake,* she improvised a dance till interrupted by one of the children's nannies, who promptly fled to Violet, reading in another room.

'Violet! Violet!' the shaken nanny cried, 'your mother is dancing in front of the new secretary, in her combinations!'

To which Violet replied coolly, 'Combinations seem a very sensible garment in which to do it.'

Stepmother and stepdaughter were clearly birds of a feather.

In May 1910 Asquith took a trip to Gibraltar to inspect the Navy. As Margot explained to her young son, who was curious about his father's departure, 'Puffin, dear, when princes and politicians need a rest they go and inspect something, preferably situated in a warm climate. Your father has gone on the Admiralty yacht to examine the defences at Gibraltar. We presumably expect a ferocious attack from a band of drink-crazed Spanish gypsy violinists.'

It proved to be a bitterly sad trip for, shortly after the yacht had passed Cadiz, the tragic news reached Asquith that Edward VII was seriously ill. Course was altered for home straight away, but at about three in the morning the Prime Minister received a wireless message announcing the King's death. He went up on deck in the half light before dawn and the first thing he saw was Halley's comet blazing in the sky. About his feelings at the time, Asquith wrote later:

I felt bewildered and indeed stunned. At a most anxious moment in the fortunes of the State, we had lost, without warning or preparation, the Sovereign whose ripe experience, trained sagacity, equitable judgement, and unvarying consideration, counted for so much. For two years I had been his Chief Minister, and I am thankful to remember that from first to last I never concealed anything from him. He soon got to know this, and in return he treated me with a gracious frankness which made our relationship in very trying and exacting times one, not always of complete agreement, but of unbroken confidence. . . . Now he had gone. His successor, with all his fine and engaging qualities, was without political experience. We were nearing the verge of a crisis almost without example in our constitutional history. What was the right thing to do? This was the question which absorbed my thoughts as we made our way, with two fast escorting cruisers, through the Bay of Biscay, until we landed at Plymouth.

Shortly after Asquith's return home to establish a relationship with the new King, George V, both Henry and Margot suffered a minor hiccup in their domestic life. As their car drew up outside Number 10 one evening following a day out, they found Downing Street full of servants rushing about, and others being interviewed by policemen.

In answer to Henry's query as to what might be happening. Margot answered in her usual way, 'This house is about as exclusive as Epsom on Derby Day! I swear if a troop of cavalry were to ride through nobody would even notice the droppings.'

But the cause of the hubbub was frightening.

Puffin and little Megan Lloyd George had been kidnapped, at least that was the interpretation Margot put on it on hearing they were missing. In such troubled times anyone could have taken them, suffragettes, anarchists, Bulgarians, they had probably been drugged by a Chinese syndicate, she thought the police should search the docks!

The police, however, were rather at a loss. As far as they could establish the children had last been seen three hours before, at about 2.00 p.m., and when they hadn't turned up for their tea a search had been instituted.

On entering Number 10, Asquith immediately noticed a change which he pointed out to everyone. The infernal and constant wheeze of a brand new lift which Margot had insisted should be put in the house to serve all floors was . . . silent!

Within seconds the missing children were found, sound asleep on the floor of the lift cage, surrounded by teddy bears and toy teacups and saucers. The lift had got stuck on the top floor and no one had bothered to search the servants' quarters.

Relieved but furious, Margot grabbed hold of Puffin and shook him like a rag doll. 'Don't you ever do that again, you wicked, wicked child!' she scolded him.

'We didn't do it on purpose, Mama,' small Puffin protested.

'And don't argue back! This is not a debate!'

In 1911 Asquith was still struggling with his Parliament Bill and he now

Margot Asquith (Dorothy Tutin) dancing in her 'combinations' to demonstrate her skills to her husband's new private secretary, Maurice Bonham Carter

Margot (Dorothy Tutin) praying with her two young children, Anthony, or 'Puffin' (Timothy Stark), and Elizabeth (Michelle Sachs), after the death of Edward VII

Henry Asquith (David Langton), 'the Last of the Romans'

went to see the new King who, like his father, suggested yet another election. But he virtually promised, this time, that two hundred and fifty to five hundred Liberal peers would be created if the problem could not be overcome by other means.

The Prime Minister went to the country, won the general election and made it known that if the Lords rejected his bill, a flood of new non-aristocratic blood would invade the Upper House.

Number 10 was now besieged by apoplectic aristocrats demanding Asquith's head. Lord Halsbury told him that any peer who voted for his poisonous bill would be expelled from his clubs and that no man would ever take him by the hand again. His friends would disown him and both socially and politically he would be ostracized. 'He would be a dead duck, Sir. Dead! Dead! Dead in the marshes!'

Lord Lansdowne warned him, 'The matter goes to the very root of the powers and pride of the nobility. It is an intensely emotive issue. It will make the House of Lords a freak, an absurdity!'

While others voiced in anger, 'It is a damnable, cursed, outrageous insult to the whole of the English aristocracy!' Henry Asquith quietly stood his ground.

Through Margot he now heard reports of peer-strewn dinner parties being held all over London, with puce-faced dukes and crimson marquises roaring at each other about private armies and military coups. Lord Halsbury got squads of whippers-in racing round town collecting reluctant peers for the vital vote in the Lords. Two of them had to be more or less winched into their seats, their legs, for all practical purposes, being too full of port to function. Backwoodsmen, who had never been in the House before in their lives, were being dragged out of hibernation, dusted off and pointed in the right direction, while Lansdowne had got three hundred and twenty peers who were prepared to abstain from voting.

The issue was balanced on the point of a needle.

On the day of the House of Lords vote, the Prime Minister with Margot and Haldane waited for the result in the drawing room of Number 10. They had heard that the Archbishop of Canterbury had made a speech in his favour that should give the bishops to Asquith, but if ever the country had need of British common sense, it was now.

After a tense hour of waiting, the telephone finally rang and Margot answered.

The news was good.

The news was victory.

They opened a bottle of champagne and drank to democracy.

But Asquith was now beset with further problems: at home, he had to contend with the Ireland Bill and the increasingly loud demands for women's suffrage; abroad, the political climate in Europe was growing

The marriage of Violet Asquith and Maurice Bonham Carter, December 1915, at Number 10 Downing Street. Asquith stands on the groom's right, and Margot on his left

dangerously unstable. In July 1914 the Hapsburg Archduke Franz Ferdinand was assassinated at Sarajevo, and there were fears that Austro-Hungary would declare war on Serbia, bringing her ally, Germany, with her. Great Britain was bound by the Triple Alliance with Russia and France, and involvement in a major conflict seemed to many to be inevitable. However Asquith wrongly saw no reason at the time why England should do anything more than be a spectator as matters escalated.

Following a Cabinet meeting on 8 July, the Prime Minister informed the King that it was his intention to prorogue Parliament in August. When Austria delivered an ultimatum to Serbia on 24 July, the Cabinet met to discuss foreign affairs for the first time in a month and, over the weekend of

25 July, decided to send a warning telegram to all naval, military and colonial stations to initiate a precautionary period. They also agreed that the Prime Minister should report to the King concerning the British attitude in the event of a German violation of Belgian territory.

Asquith wrote to George V:

The Cabinet consider that this matter, if it arises, will be rather one of policy than of legal obligation. . . . After much discussion it was agreed that Sir E. Grey should be authorized to inform the German and French ambassadors that at this stage we were unable to pledge ourselves in advance, either under all conditions to stand aside or in any conditions join in.

By 30 July the situation had worsened and Asquith was concerned by 'the terrible state of depression and paralysis of opinion in the City' coupled with a desire to keep out of the possible conflict at all costs.

France then started to apply pressure in the form of moral blackmail, and the crisis escalated. A few days later, after several urgent Cabinet meetings, Asquith noted with distaste the beginnings of war hysteria outside Number 10. 'There were large crowds perambulating the streets and cheering the King at Buckingham Palace and one could hear the distant roaring as late as 1 or 1.30 in the morning. War, or anything that seems likely to lead to war is always popular with the London mob. One remembers Sir R. Walpole's remark "Now they are ringing their bells; in a few weeks they'll be wringing their hands." How one loathes such levity.'

On 4 August the news came through that German troops had invaded Belgium and an ultimatum, to expire at midnight, was issued to the German Government. The Prime Minister was confident that he would be able to cope with the conflict to come. He was healthy and less tired than many of his ministers, whom he considered to be overtaxed. 'The whole prospect fills me with sadness,' he wrote, but having managed through six unceasing years of problems, he didn't believe one more, however great, would undo him.

Margot wrote about the endless evening of waiting for the ultimatum to expire:

I looked at the children asleep after dinner before joining Henry in the Cabinet Room. Lord Crewe and Sir Edward Grey were already there and we sat smoking cigarettes in silence; some went out, others came in; nothing was said. The clock on the mantelpiece hammered out the hour, and when the last beat of midnight struck, it was as silent as dawn. We were at War. I left to go to bed and, as I was pausing at the foot of the staircase I saw Winston Churchill with a happy face striding towards the double doors of the Cabinet Room.

Even in reporting this historic event, Margot allowed herself an hour's literary licence, for the clocks were ahead in Berlin and the ultimatum had come into force at 11.00 p.m. in London.

Henry and Margot

In May 1915 Asquith formed a coalition Government which included Arthur James Balfour, who became First Lord of the Admiralty, and Andrew Bonar Law who became Colonial Secretary. Lord Kitchener was appointed War Minister and David Lloyd George Minister of Munitions. But it was not successful. As the war started to claim unprecedentedly heavy losses, so the Government became unpopular. Asquith was accused of weakness and self-interest and the press turned against him.

1916 proved a year of tragedy for Asquith. In Dublin the Irish republicans declared Ireland independent in the short-lived Easter Rising; Lord Kitchener was drowned on his way to Russia; then came the September push on the Somme, which proved a disaster with thousands of young men being needlessly slaughtered, among them Raymond Asquith, Henry's eldest son.

On Sunday September 17th, we were entertaining a weekend party [Margot wrote later]. While we were playing tennis in the afternoon my husband went for a drive with my cousin, Nan Tennant. He looked well, and had been delighted with his recent visit to the front. As it was my little son's last Sunday before going back to Winchester I told him he might run across from the Barn in his pyjamas after dinner and sit with us while the men were in the dining room. While we were playing games, Clouder, our servant, came in to say that I was wanted. I left the room and the moment I took up the telephone I said to myself 'Raymond is killed.' With the receiver in my hand, I asked what it was, and if the news was bad. Our secretary, Davies, answered, 'Terrible, terrible news. Raymond was shot dead on the 15th. Haig writes full of sympathy, but no details. The Guards went in and he was shot leading his men the moment he had gone over the parapet. 'I put back the receiver and sat down. I heard Elizabeth's delicious laugh, and a hum of talk and smell of cigars came down the passage from the dining room. I went back into the sitting room. 'Raymond is dead,' I said. 'He was shot leading his men over the top on Friday.' Puffin got up from his game and hanging his head took my hand; Elizabeth burst into tears. . . . Maud Tree and Flotty Bridges suggested I should put off telling Henry the terrible news as he was happy. I walked away with the two children and rang the bell; 'Tell the Prime Minister to come and speak to me,' I said to the servant. Leaving the children I paused at the end of the dining room passage; Henry opened the door and we stood facing each other. He saw my thin white face, and while he put his arm round me I said 'Terrible, terrible news.' At this he stopped me and said, 'I know, I've known it . . . Raymond is dead.' He put his hands over his face and we walked into an empty room and sat down in silence.

The Asquiths were grief-stricken, but the newspapers, after a moment's pause, campaigned on against Henry, and Margot did not help. She did not seem to grasp the full meaning of the war, despite Raymond's death. On one occasion she naively mentioned that whatever it all meant it would not stop her liking the Germans. When she paid a visit to a German prisoner of war camp, the press was intensely critical and made even more of rumours that Asquith had become rich with shares in Krupps, the German armaments firm, and that Elizabeth had become engaged to marry a German general.

Henry Asquith in 1922. He had turned to writing in the hope of emulating his wife's success

Margot, alas, did little to change these attitudes. She would not join in good works with other ladies for the war effort. She had never become involved in such things, and still believed that the poor were there to be patronized and preached to about drinking too much gin.

When Lloyd George replaced Kitchener as War Minister in 1916, Margot saw this as the end of her husband's leadership. 'We are out,' she wrote. 'It can only be a question of time now before we have to leave Downing Street.'

She voiced her intense dislike for Lloyd George, which was not always wise, for he could give back as much as he got. 'Lloyd George cannot see a belt without hitting below it,' was one of her comments. 'Put Lloyd George in a room by himself and he would shrivel up and disappear,' was another.

Lloyd George himself simply commented, 'Mrs Asquith is silly, miserable and buzzing about like a mosquito in the room with her wings bedraggled but her sting active and indiscriminate.'

As the year came to an end, Lloyd George suggested that a small war committee should be formed, which would enjoy full powers, subject to the supreme control of the Prime Minister, to direct all questions connected with the war. It was political manoeuvring by Lloyd George, and after many open and secretive discussions among the Cabinet Ministers, Asquith agreed that there should be such a War Committee under Lloyd George's chairmanship, operating with the safeguard that the Prime Minister was to have supreme and effective control of war policy.

When *The Times* published an insulting article criticizing him for taking a subordinate post to Lloyd George, Asquith changed his mind. Lloyd George therefore resigned, the Liberals stuck to Asquith, but the Conservatives backed the War Minister, and Asquith's resignation was called for.

On 5 December 1916 he resigned. He stayed out of office for the rest of the war and in 1918 even lost his East Fife seat in the General Election, having held it for thirty-two years.

The Liberal Party blamed him for their loss of power and, though he won a by-election at Paisley six years later as an Independent Liberal, returning triumphantly to the House of Commons, the atmosphere in politics had changed and no longer suited him.

When the Asquiths first moved out of Number 10, they lived for a short period in Cavendish Square, but then were forced to sell the house through shortage of money, and took up residence in Bedford Square in cheaper Bloomsbury. Margot decided to earn an income by writing and her autobiography was published in 1920. It was a best-seller because it was as indiscreet as it was inaccurate. Though it appalled her friends and everyone in the family but Henry, its sales encouraged her to write other books in the same vein. Seeing her successful in this field and knowing that Winston Churchill had bought Chartwell on the proceeds of his writings,

UP THE POPLAR TREE.

Mr. Asquith. "I WONDER WHETHER GLADSTONE WOULD HAVE SPARED THIS TREE."

Asquith as leader of the Independent Liberals, wondering whether to try to bring down the government. From Punch, *27 February 1924*

Henry Asquith set pen to paper as well, but not very successfully.

In 1924 he was created an Earl, calling himself the Earl of Oxford and Asquith. This raised a few eyebrows among the die-hard Lords, one of whom suggested that it was rather like a suburban villa calling itself Versailles.

Two years later Asquith suffered a stroke which caused him the sudden loss of power in one leg. He recovered for a while, but had to take to a wheelchair, which he found demoralizing. He suffered a hardening of the arteries and, though there was an improvement by the end of the year, he suffered a relapse and his mind started to wander. He died peacefully the following February and Margot, who found it hard to live with failure and suffering, was visibly relieved.

She herself lived on till the beginning of the Second World War, defying old age by always dressing beautifully, holding soirées and entertaining as she had all her life. She leant more and more towards the arts helped by her son Anthony who was now a famous film director. It is, perhaps, by a famous film business quote that she will be best remembered. Explaining the pronunciation of her name to Jean Harlow, she said, 'The "t" is silent as in Harlow.'

CHAPTER SIX

A Woman of Style

David Lloyd George became Prime Minister in the middle of the First World War. He was a turbulent man for turbulent times, and his troublesome private life was spent torn between two determined women – his wife and his mistress.

His father, William George, a Pembrokeshire schoolmaster, died in 1864 when David was just over a year old. His mother, unable to earn a living with two small children and expecting a third, had no alternative but to leave Bwlford where they were living on a farm and move in with her brother's family at Llanystumdwy, some hundred or so miles to the north. It was here, in the small Caernarvon village, that young George grew up.

His uncle, Richard Lloyd, was a cobbler running a small shoemaking business. A radical lay preacher, he took it upon himself to bring up David who, it was clear, was alert with a very bright mind. At school he excelled in mathematics and showed promise in public speaking, so that a legal career was decided on, but this meant he had to have a working knowledge of Latin and French. Neither subject was taught at this school, so his uncle set to and spent hours with him teaching him both languages, which were truly foreign to him as well.

In 1877, when he was fourteen, David went to Liverpool to sit for the Preliminary Law Examination, which he passed, enabling him to join a firm of solicitors as an apprentice at Portmadoc, a picturesque seaport town six miles from his home. At the end of a six-month trial period his employers were satisfied with his progress and he was appointed an articled clerk to the junior partner for a period of five years.

By 1884 he had passed all the necessary legal exams to set up practice on his own, which he did in Criccieth, a neighbouring town, working from a back parlour and also from similar branch offices in Portmadoc and Blaenau Ffestiniog.

David Lloyd George's childhood home at Llanystumdwy in Caernarvonshire

The going was hard to begin with, trying to gain recognition, and in a diary entry for January 1885 he recorded, 'Not a soul called to see whether I was alive or dead.' But things improved gradually and towards the end of the following month he wrote. 'First week in County Court. Won a boring case at Pwllheli after a long sharp fight. Several cases at Portmadoc.' By June he was happier, noting, 'Won all my cases. Pentrefelin trespass case very hard fought, but won on a point of law.'

He first made a real name for himself over a strange and sinister case involving the burial of an old quarryman who wanted to be laid to rest next to his daughter's grave. The local rector refused to have the man buried in his churchyard on the grounds that he was a disbeliever, so the deceased's friends went to Lloyd George for advice. He told them to bury the man regardless, which they did after dark, and the rector took them to court and won his case. Lloyd George appealed, the County Court ruled for the rector. Lloyd George appealed again and eventually at the High Court of Justice in London he won, making full use of his eloquent powers of persuasion.

It was at about this time that he met Margaret Owen, the daughter of strict Methodists who ran a farm of a hundred acres on the hill above Criccieth. Though the mother could hardly sign her name and the father was poorly educated, they were worthy citizens with a comparatively good standard of living. There was no electricity or gas in the house, the bedrooms were icy cold, but they survived on more than turnips, potatoes or bread and dripping, the staple diet of many of their neighbours.

Margaret was the only child, doted on, but brought up firmly. She worked in the house with her mother and a maid who came in daily, and on one occasion she was disciplined with birch twigs for daring to whistle on a Sunday. She was sent to a boarding school at Barmouth, some thirty miles to the south, making the journey home by train at weekends to be with her parents.

She was eighteen when she and David Lloyd George met and he wrote in his diary, ' She is a sensible girl without any fuss or affectation about her,' then later, 'She seems to be a jollier girl as you get on with her.'

The Owens did not think the young struggling solicitor suitable for their daughter. He had the reputation of being proudly anti-establishment, besides which he dressed flashily and cheaply. They did not beat about the bush, therefore, but simply forbade Margaret to see him, which only made the young man more determined to captivate her.

Secretly they wrote each other love letters which they left in a hole in the farm wall, and whenever the Owens were away he sneaked up to the house to see her.

They had one ally, Margiad the maid, who was devoted to Margaret, though to begin with she sent Lloyd George packing. 'We don't want no Baptists round our farm, go back to the girls of Llanystumdwy! ' To which he retorted, 'Now be sensible Margiad. Just do me the favour of telling Maggie Owen that I can kiss better than those Calvinist louts. Tell her you know because I've tried it on you!'

The romance blossomed despite the Owens' disapproval, and David's own family, who hardly rejoiced at the idea of his getting married at all at this stage of his career – and worse to a Methodist – was powerless to influence him.

But Margaret was not all he had on his mind. Lloyd George made his first move towards a political career when asked to address a meeting of farmers and welcome the guest of honour, Michael Davitt, who had created the Land League in Ireland in 1879. David's welcoming speech was so impressive that Davitt advised him to think seriously of going into politics, and within a month the young solicitor was sounding out local opinion as to what support he would get.

By now his brother William had passed his law exams and joined him to form Lloyd George & George, Solicitors, establishing themselves respectably in Criccieth High Street. This, together with his growing reputation as an eloquent speaker in the Portmadoc debating society, sermons in various chapels and journalistic contributions in local newspapers, changed the Owens' attitude towards him.

He proposed, but Margaret hesitated.

His persuasive blue eyes and handsome dark looks were the problem. She just did not trust him, suspecting him of being a flirt and philanderer, and told him so outright.

So he wrote to her, 'Which would you prefer, a namby pamby who would always be hanging at the hem of your petticoat, or a real demon, though he would sometimes lose his temper with you? Tell me the truth Maggie.'

He knew her to be fascinated by his streak of wildness and was gambling on that attraction, but he had to overcome an unexpected setback. Rumour spread locally that he was having an affair with a young girl he had just defended in a breach of promise action. Margaret wrote him an icy note suggesting that he had made a mistake and that his proposal had obviously been to the wrong girl.

Furious, he wrote back, 'I have made my choice, I must ask you to make yours. We must settle this miserable squabble once and for all.'

The squabble was duly settled and she accepted his proposal. They were married in January 1888 in a small chapel some five miles from Criccieth. His mother, sister and brother did not attend the wedding but Richard Lloyd, his uncle, carried out the ceremony with a Calvinist minister, a compromise which apparently satisfied all parties.

David and Margaret then caught a train for London, where they spent ten days' honeymoon which went well until the last hour when, at Euston Station, the cabman who had taken them there demanded a larger tip than Lloyd George thought he deserved. Both men had a heated argument, which nearly resulted in a fist fight, Lloyd George taking off his coat and handing it to Margaret, who screamed at him tearfully not to get involved.

The unsettled couple travelled silently back to Criccieth, where, fortunately, they were welcomed warmly by the family. They were taken up to the Owens' farm, where it had been agreed they would live till they were financially secure to buy their own home.

After a few months, the new bridegroom started to find married life a trifle tedious and, making the excuse that a future politician and successful solicitor should socialize more to gain useful contacts, he joined the local dramatic society, enabling him to get out in the evenings. During early rehearsals he met a wealthy widow named Mrs Jones whose attractions he singularly failed to resist. Margaret had suspected him of being a flirt and philanderer; her fears were proved correct, a fact with which she would have to live for the rest of her life.

Later the same year the Local Government Act was passed, resulting in the creation of county councils, and the first elections were held in 1889. Lloyd George was invited to stand for Caernarvon County Council, but he declined, being far more ambitious. He campaigned furiously for the Liberal Party, however, and, according to the *Caernarvon Herald*, 'made a hit which was vociferously cheered when he said that rivers were being kept as a sort of preserve for the aristocracy and that trout and salmon were considered to be too sacred to be on the tables of the common people'.

Margaret gave birth to a baby boy that same year and settled down to the happy family life which she had worked for, yet could not fully enjoy. Whatever David might get up to beyond the boundaries of the farm began to

David Lloyd George (John Stride), the Welsh Wizard

The two women in Lloyd George's life: his wife Margaret (Rhoda Lewis); and his secretary Frances Stevenson (Barbara Kellermann)

David Lloyd George (John Stride) with his mistress Frances Stevenson (Barbara Kellermann)

be less important. If she could control her pride then she could tolerate his silly behaviour.

But the following March, as they were all preparing to go away on a short holiday, she heard the shattering news that the kindly old gentleman who represented Caernarvon at Westminster had suddenly died of a heart attack, which meant that David would stand as Liberal candidate at the by-election. As expected, he immediately abandoned the idea of going away with his wife and child, and instead burnt the midnight oil writing his election address, which was published on 24 March and ran to nearly six hundred words.

Recent by-elections [it read] prove that the country is sick and tired of Mr Balfour's baton-and-bayonet rule in Ireland, and of his desperate attempts to repress by martial law legitimate aspirations of a generous nation. I come before you as a firm believer in and admirer of Mr Gladstone's noble alternative of Justice in Ireland. Whilst fully recognizing that the wrongs of Ireland must of necessity have the first claim upon the attention of the Liberal Party, I am deeply impressed with the fact that Wales has wants and aspirations of her own which have too long been ignored, but which must no longer be neglected. First and foremost among these, stands the cause of religious Liberty and Equality in Wales. If returned to Parliament by you, it shall be my earnest endeavour to labour for the triumph of this great cause.

Margaret, who was expecting her second child, prayed that nothing would come of it. 'I had thought,' she told a friend, 'that I was marrying a Caernarvonshire lawyer. The shadow of the election is spoiling everything, the sunshine has gone out my day.' She worried that if her husband won, her life would become intolerable, for however much he might be highly regarded, he would also be an impoverished MP.

David himself, together with his supporters was not sure of the outcome of the elections, but at the end of polling day on 10 April 1890, after an unexpected recount, he learned that he had won by a narrow majority of 18 in a total poll of 4,000.

David Lloyd George was a Member of Parliament.

Seated in a carriage drawn through Caernarvon, he was cheered as 'The Boy MP'. He wanted to go home immediately, but was told that his supporters in Bangor had to see him and there was no point in arguing, so he stopped there. Eventually he reached Criccieth in the evening and was greeted by a vast multitude wild with excitement and a welcoming committee who insisted on pulling him up the hill in an open cart to the Owens' farm, celebrating the conquering hero's triumph. Bonfires were lit, houses were bright with light, a torchlight procession followed his progress to the accompaniment of shouting and singing which could be heard across Cardigan Bay.

Margaret, watching the exuberant crowd from the farmhouse door with her parents, could not hide her anxiety for the future and, when David reached the gate, she contained herself no longer. Turning on her heels she ran to the safety of her bedroom and sent the nurse out to hush the merrymakers. 'What is all this going on? Do you want to wake the baby?'

Stunned and subdued by this deadly reception, Lloyd George stepped into his in-laws' house, turned to wave at his joyful supporters and closed the door.

If, in later years, he had need to excuse his infidelity, it was perhaps at this moment that Margaret had handed him one, for Lloyd George believed that a woman's main role in a marriage was to sympathize and soothe the husband, and he expected his wife to regard him as Number One, to fuss over him when he felt unwell, to feed him what he wanted when he wanted, putting his needs before her own. Margaret, however, had a strong will of her own and now, as in the future, was to refuse to submit to the 'Master'.

When he told her that with his Membership of Parliament they would go and live in London, she told him that he would be going alone. Pregnant, she considered that the capital would be unhealthy both for her and the newborn and that if Lloyd George's new career demanded him to be there, he would have to make the sacrifice of living without her. So he left Criccieth, sad that she would not share this moment of glory.

Lloyd George's victory was confirmation for the Liberal Party that the tide of public opinion was changing in their favour. The Conservatives under Lord Salisbury had been in office for four years, other by-elections were coming up with similar results and Gladstone, in the wings, was getting ready for a come-back. He duly won the 1892 election but resigned two years later and was succeeded as Prime Minister by Lord Rosebery. The Conservatives were returned in 1895, again under Lord Salisbury, but during all this time the 'Welsh Wizard', as Lloyd George came to be nick-named, proved he was someone to be reckoned with. He disliked the Tory MPs, and all they stood for, so much that he angled for opportunities when he could lacerate them and their snobbery and make fun of them with damaging wit, which caused many to hesitate tackling him in debates.

Nevertheless his private life was of course lonely. He lived in one room at the Liberal Club, subsidized his poor MP's income by working as a part-time solicitor helping out his brother William, while Margaret, who had given birth to a daughter Mair, lived on with her family in Wales. He wanted her to be with him, and eventually managed to get an apartment in the Grays Inn Road which would be suitable for all of them. But she still refused to come up to London for any length of time, and when she did she pointedly left the children behind.

'There is a great difference,' he wrote to her in Wales, 'between being cramped up in a suffocating malodorous chapel listening to superstitious rot, and having a ride in the fresh air on the river.' He had come to hate Criccieth with its small-minded atmosphere.

Restless, he moved into a flat in Kensington and out again because it was too expensive. Margaret, now with four children, continued living on the farm, but she started getting involved in politics, having discovered that her husband had a pathological dislike of opening letters and was thus proving a bad constituency MP.

Learning to nurse his local supporters she helped him to retain his popularity and he encouraged her continually. 'You must make a good speech, that will surprise them. I am sure you can do it. You have any quantity of brains of a very good quality if you only set them to work. Think, that is what you must do.'

In London his past unexpectedly caught up with him when a certain Mrs Edwards, a Monmouthshire doctor's wife, petitioned for a divorce. Rumours had abounded that she had had an affair with Lloyd George and had even borne his child. Now the whole business threatened to become public in a court case which involved him as a solicitor and his political career was in jeopardy. Fortunately, he managed to escape being directly mentioned, though his name came up in *The Times*, and those who could read between the lines gathered that he might not have been totally innocent. Margaret was once more patient and accepted the promises he made to reform, though he pointed out that had any of the accusations been true, they would have been true of something in the past and long forgotten.

When the House of Commons was sitting, Margaret occasionally joined him in London for short periods, scurrying back to beloved Wales when she was satisfied that he could look after himself. But Lloyd George was quite incapable of resisting a pretty face, and when a young and attractive lady crossed his path he again became entangled. This time it was the young wife of one of his loyal supporters, Tim Davis, the President of the Welsh Presbyterian Association. The couple lived in Fulham and it became customary for Lloyd George to stroll over to their house with his children while Margaret prepared the Sunday roast – when his family was in London – and to stroll over more often when it wasn't.

Tim Davies, an older man, seemed content to leave his young wife in the company of the MP he respected, and inevitably the friendship blossomed. Just as inevitably, with children around, they were discovered. One morning, Richard, Lloyd George's little son, reported to his mother that he had seen 'Daddy eating Mrs Davies's hand', which he thought peculiar. Margaret instantly realized the total extent of the meal and found it preferable to return to Wales, from where she wrote her erring husband a scathing letter complaining about their relationship and demanding an explanation as to why he found it necessary, as he so often did, to remain in London when the House was in recess. 'This business comes between you and me more so than you imagine, and is growing, and you know it, yet you cannot shake it off. It pains me to the quick and I am very unhappy. If you must go on as at present I don't know where it will end. Beware you don't give place for any scandal for the sake of your own personal self and your bright career.'

Lloyd George's reaction was naturally fiercely defensive:

What a jealous little wife I have to be sure. Your letter this morning made me wild. There was the same self complacent Pharisaism about it as ever. Be candid with yourself and reflect whether you have not rather neglected your husband. I have scores of times come home in the dead of night to a cold, dark, comfortless flat. You have been a good mother. You have not – and I say this now not in anger – not always been a good wife.

This time Margaret took no further chances and agreed to come back to London with all the children to stay for good. The family moved into a house near Wandsworth Common, its first real London home, and in return for this gesture the Mrs Tim Davies affair was at an end.

In the Wandsworth house the Lloyd Georges' way of life was to be established. Once through the door you were in Wales, indeed in Criccieth, for no English was spoken and anyone living there, from servants to temporary builders and painters, were from the little Welsh town. Cider and lemonade were the only drinks ever served at table and when he wanted to entertain guests with more sophistication, Lloyd George would have to connive with the maid to get whisky smuggled in. He would go to great lengths to hide such skulduggery, as he would to cover up his lapses in attending church on Sundays.

When the Boer War broke out in 1899 Lloyd George took a firm stand against it, not wanting Britain to side with the greedy goldminers against a small state like the Transvaal. He toured Britain attacking the Government's policy, causing a serious riot in Birmingham, the constituency of Joseph Chamberlain, the Colonial Secretary. Though it was supposedly a private Liberal meeting, the Chamberlainites stormed the town hall armed with bricks and sticks. Efforts by the police to keep out the roughs proved useless, and before Lloyd George could get up and speak, the place was packed with seven thousand people, most of whom were waving Union Jacks, blowing trumpets and singing *Rule Britannia* to make sure the Welshman would not be heard.

Never one to be daunted, he stood up and took his coat off, then addressed the rabble. 'This is rather a lively meeting for a peace meeting,' he started, but never finished. Within minutes fights had broken out, Lloyd George had to be escorted out, and left the building disguised as a policeman while others on the platform made their escape as best they could. Hearing that their man had got away, the angry rioters stormed the hall, resulting in one policeman and one of the mob being killed and at least forty people injured.

David Lloyd George, rising Liberal politican, with his wife, Margaret, and his daughters, Megan (left) and Mair (right), in 1904. Mair was to die of appendicitis at the tragically early age of seventeen, a bitter blow to her parents

Lloyd George had not made his speech, but he had left his mark on Chamberlain's constituency.

In 1906 the Liberals came back to power under Sir Henry Campbell-Bannerman, and Lloyd George was appointed President of the Board of Trade. As such he established the Port of London Authority and was successful in averting a threatened dock strike.

Parliament was his life and his family's life, and he behaved himself, putting all his energies into his work for the good of the country. Peace, however, was not to grace the household for long. Tragedy struck when Mair, his pretty seventeen-year-old daughter, died of appendicitis which could so easily have been treated. Working hard for forthcoming exams, she had suffered stomach pains in silence in order not to waste valuable time, and the danger was discovered too late.

For several weeks after her death Lloyd George was a broken man, and his closest friends and colleagues actually feared for his sanity. Eventually he recovered sufficiently to take his sons for a holiday in the South of France while Margaret coped with a move from Wandsworth to Cheyne Place in Chelsea. Neither of them wanted to remain in a house filled with the bitterly sad memories of Mair.

In 1908 Sir Henry Campbell-Bannerman died and Asquith took office as Prime Minister. He appointed Lloyd George as Chancellor of the Exchequer and the whole family moved again, this time to Number 11 Downing Street. Lloyd George, still haunted by Mair's death and unable to accustom himself to the idea that she could not share his success, nearly suffered a relapse. Thankfully he had Margaret to lean on, who proved much the stronger and threw herself body and soul into reorganizing their routine and supervising, among other things, the building of a new house above Criccieth which would be named Brynawelon.

The move to Number 11 Downing Street was a happy one. With Lloyd George too busy to misbehave, she felt more secure. But she also loved the house which had a country feel, with its labyrinth of passages, cosy bedrooms at the back, and a small drawing room on the first floor which had a low enough ceiling to give an impression that it was in a cottage rather than in an official government residence.

Now middle-aged, Margaret was a stoutish, motherly woman, good humoured but placid, and never too keen on housework, let alone cooking. Fortunately Sarah Jones, their housekeeper, was there to take care of all the chores. Both women quickly turned the place into what friends regarded as the Welsh Embassy, for the family talked Welsh amongst themselves and the three maids below stairs were also Welsh speaking.

Margaret spent a good deal of her time in the garden, and though she never expected to grow anything in London as well as she could in Criccieth, it was better than nothing.

Lloyd George first introduced the outgoing Chancellor, Asquith's, budget, giving pensions to those over the age of seventy. He then introduced his own 'People's Budget', which he claimed was a war budget, waged against poverty. He intended to spend millions on old age pensions, labour exchanges, national parks and roads, all to be paid for by taxing land and increasing death duties. For seventy-three days and many nights the debates went on. Margaret, now fully involved in his life, sat up in the gallery listening to her husband attacking and being attacked, then walked back with him across Whitehall in the early hours.

The whole budget turmoil suited Lloyd George, who attacked the big landlords in an inflammatory speech down in the East End, in Limehouse. The case against 'the dukes', as he called the landowners, was that their income had increased enormously by no exertion at all. 'You have got a system in this country whereby landlords take advantage of the fact that they have got control of the land to let it for a number of years and at the end the whole of it passes away to pockets of men who never spent a penny on it.'On another occasion he thundered out the question, 'Who's going to rule the country? The King and the Peers, or the King and the People?' This resulted in the King himself writing to Asquith, suggesting that his Chancellor should leave his name out of politics.

But scandal struck once more when *The People* Sunday newspaper printed a story hinting that the Chancellor of the Exchequer might soon be named as co-respondent in another divorce case and that frantic efforts were being made to keep the business quiet. Lloyd George was forced to sue for libel and, to make sure he would win the case, he begged Margaret to appear with him in Court. 'One day I shall be Prime Minister. If you help me you shall never regret your decision.'

Margaret's loyalty and protective generosity saved the day, and once he had appeared in the witness box denying all the allegations, the newspaper admitted the libel charges and apologized with a cheque for £1,000, which was sent to Llanystumdwy towards the building of a village institute.

Lloyd George then promptly fell in love again, this time with Frances Stevenson, a twenty-three-year-old teacher at a Wimbledon girls' boarding school. She had been in the same class as Mair and, apparently, looked a little like her.

Both Margaret and he had decided that Megan, their youngest daughter aged nine, should go to a boarding school in the autumn, but that she needed extra coaching before doing so. After a number of possible tutors had applied, Frances was summoned for an interview at Number 11. She was surprised to be taken through a door to Number 10 by the butler, who then explained that as Mr Asquith was upstairs in the drawing room, Mr Lloyd George would see her in the Prime Minister's study which he much preferred to his own.

THE PHILANTHROPIC HIGHWAYMAN.

Mr. Lloyd-George. "*I'LL MAKE 'EM PITY THE AGED POOR!*"

David Lloyd George as the new Chancellor of the Exchequer in 1908. First he introduced the budget of his predecessor, Asquith, giving pensions to those over seventy, but then he planned to put forward his 'People's budget', declaring war on poverty

The interview started off on fairly familiar terms, though Miss Stevenson was nervous and felt more like one of her own pupils being examined by a headmaster. Fascinated by her, Lloyd George straight away switched on the legendary charm and flirted with her, guessing her age to be twenty. She corrected him and he jokingly reprimanded her, 'Very well then, make me a liar for three years, I don't care. Bonar Law now, he hates being called a liar. I don't mind a bit. Have you heard the latest rhyme about me?' She was not sure which one he meant, there were quite a few going the rounds.

Lloyd George no doubt, when his life ebbs out,
Will ride on a flaming chariot,
Seated in state on a red hot plate
'Twixt Satan and Judas Iscariot,
Ananias that day to the Devil will say
'My claim for precedence fails
So move me up higher, away from the fire
And make way for that liar – from Wales!

When she said she thought the rhyme disrespectful, she delighted him even more. Lloyd George engaged her immediately, packing her off to Brynawelon as soon as she could go, where she was received by Margaret and Megan.

To his daughter he wrote a while later, 'I am glad you like your new companion and that you get on so well together. I knew you would. I want you to learn French like a petite Parisian and play the piano like Paderewski.'

Frances became one of the family and over the whole of August, when Lloyd George was dutifully at home, she had a wonderful time accompanying them on many excursions, picnics and days by the seaside.

One afternoon on such a picnic party, the Lloyd George children, Richard, Olwen, Gwylm and Megan, in the company of Margaret and Frances, were treated to a display of legs by their father, Winston Churchill then president of the Board of Trade, and Max Aitken, later Lord Beaverbrook.

The latter two, while walking barefoot in a stream, had claimed sturdier calves than Lloyd George and, calling for a tape measure, he insisted that Frances should measure each of them. The request was very personal and intimate, and though she complied, announcing that the Chancellor's calf was half an inch more in diameter than those of his rivals, she was very aware of the disdain with which Margaret looked upon the proceedings.

Later still, in a dangerously intimate mood, Lloyd George told her he required a secretary, a *private* secretary and, getting the drift of his request, she rejected the idea, reminding him of his family. 'My family has nothing to do with it,' he protested, then, smiling, allowed himself a typical burst of eloquence:

David Lloyd George, 'seated in state on a red hot plate 'twixt Satan and Judas Iscariot'

Lloyd George's mistress, Frances Stevenson, at her desk in Number 10

Frances, *cariad*, listen to me. I need you. Like this grass needs the rain. My mind meshes with yours. It never has with Margaret's. She's not interested in power, in the levers that move men's lives. You are. It won't be a picnic. There's a terrible time coming. Winston can see it. And so can I. The Germans, the road hogs of Europe, will have war. I will be asked to smash them. Asquith will have to go. I can do it, but I must have a girl I love with me. Why, girl, it's practically your duty to your country!

Frances, flattered but cautious, agreed to become his secretary, but made no other promises.

In the Commons Lloyd George persisted with his attacks on the rich. In 1912 his National Insurance Bill became law, making insurance against sickness and unemployment compulsory for manual workers. He was now recognized as a great social reformer and a most radical Liberal.

As the year 1914 approached and the clouds of unrest gathered in Europe, Asquith relied on him more and more. He was sent to Ireland to try to calm down the warring factions, and he settled a serious railway strike at home.

One morning in June he opened a despatch box from the Foreign Office and read that Archduke Ferdinand, the heir to the Austro-Hungarian throne, had been assassinated at Sarajevo. Unlike others he was not particularly alarmed. 'This means war,' he said to Frances, but he was not thinking in terms of a major confrontation. Six days later, in fact, he addressed the Commons claiming that there was an improvement in Anglo-German relations:

Our relations are very much better than they were a few years ago. There is none of that snarling which we used to see, more especially in the Press of those two great, I will not say rival nations, but two great Empires. The feeling is altogether better between them. They begin to realize they can co-operate for common ends, and that the points of co-operation are greater and more numerous and more important than the points of possible controversy. All that is to the good.

He was wrong, however, for on 4 August, war was declared.

He immediately closed the Stock Exchange to stop panic selling, replacing gold sovereigns with Treasury notes and organizing schemes to bring in money for armaments. Asquith appointed him Minister of Munitions and with his enormous energy he spurred anyone and everyone to work for the war effort, making a speech in Parliament criticizing the lethargy in both management and men working in the war industry:

Too late in moving here! Too late in arriving there! Too late in coming to this decision! Too late in starting with enterprises! Too late in preparing! In this war the footsteps of the Allies have been dogged by the mocking spectre of 'Too Late', and unless we quicken our movements, damnation will fall on the sacred cause for which so much gallant blood has flowed. I beg employers and workmen not to have 'Too Late' inscribed upon the portals of their workshops!

By 1916 the war was going badly and Lloyd George was getting impatient with his superiors, fully aware that they had old-fashioned attitudes and were entering battle campaigns as if against Napoleon a century before.

In June Lord Kitchener, Secretary for War, perished when the ship in which he was travelling to Russia hit a mine and sank with virtually all on board. 'What a tragedy,' Lloyd George wrote. 'Poor Kitchener died at the best moment for the country and for him. I used to get on well with Kitchener. Great driving force but no mental powers. That is my reading of him. Hard eyes, relentlessness, without a glimmer of human kindness.'

Lloyd George was appointed War Minister in his stead and started pushing harder than ever. Though he admired Asquith as a Prime Minister in peace-time, he had his doubts as to his leadership in war. And things got worse. On the first day of the Somme offensive 57,000 men were lost and many more were to be killed in the months that followed. Lloyd George could not stand Asquith's policies any longer and suggested he should head a small War Committee of which Asquith would not be a member. The Prime Minister agreed, but when accused by *The Times* of taking a back seat at a time of crisis, he withdrew his agreement.

Lloyd George thereupon resigned, but, much to his surprise, Asquith also resigned, and George V sent for the Conservative opposition leader, Bonar Law, asking him to form a government. Bonar Law declined, stating that only one man could pull Britain through the war and that was Lloyd George.

On 7 December 1916 he therefore became Prime Minister, heading a Coalition Government. Once more the Lloyd George family was on the move, but this time only through the door leading from Number 11 to Number 10. Margaret's, Richard's, Olwen's, Gwylm's and Megan's belongings, then Frances Stevenson's secretarial desk and office equipment, made the small but momentous move.

As Prime Minister Lloyd George did not change either his way of life or his morals. He read himself to sleep with Wild West stories and penny dreadfuls, awoke at 4.30 in the morning, calling for the newspapers and his breakfast at 7.00. Sarah Jones went on serving him frizzled bacon and chips for breakfast, lunch and high tea, while he expected Margaret, Megan and Frances to be at his beck and call. Though he was not really hopeless in organizing his life, he often indulged in the pretence, claiming it impossible to tie a tie, find a book or even sometimes to open a door.

Number 10 now became as much a War Office as a home, private life merging with politics, diplomacy and campaigning against the Germans. Having sworn his family and servants to secrecy, Lloyd George openly discussed vital State matters at the breakfast or luncheon table with whomever cared to join for a meal, and the talk could switch from one subject to another with anyone joining in.

David Lloyd George, recently appointed War Minister by Asquith, preparing for his new role. Cartoon from the Western Mail

On one occasion, when Winston Churchill and Max Aitken were again his guests, Churchill launched into one of his attacks on General Haig. 'The Germans,' he said, 'have two fearsome weapons – the submarine and General Haig. The one destroys our ships and our food, the other pours away our life's blood in the trenches.'

Aitken suggested that if British tanks were used the German centre would be rolled up like a carpet, but Lloyd George pointed out that General Haig's toffee-nosed cavalry would scream that they would not be turned into chauffeurs. Army traditions, among other things, were becoming a major problem to deal with. The Prime Minister then looked up from his plate and asked irritably, 'Does anyone know what today is?'

One of his sons suggested it might be the anniversary of the Gallipoli massacre, but it was not that. 'It's my bloody birthday, that's what it is!' he ranted. 'Not a "happy birthday", not a present, not even a card! Here am I,

Lloyd George's closest political allies during the First World War: Max Aitken, later to become Lord Beaverbrook; and Winston Churchill, seen here with Lloyd George on Budget Day, 1910

Prime Minister of the greatest nation on earth, fighting a war to save mankind, and I'm not even worth a bit of cardboard to anyone!'

Margaret and the children apologized in turn, admitting that they had completely forgotten, but Churchill went on with his own train of thought, 'We must staunch both haemorrhages. You must get rid of Haig and build more ships.' 'And there's another thing too,' Lloyd George responded. 'Someone closed my bedroom window last night. I've got a head this morning like a stuffed marrow. I'm just not considered in this house,' to which Sarah Jones answered tartly as she cleared the dishes, 'Goodness me! We'll be complaining soon that someone stole our teddy bear!'

Megan, now aged fourteen, rushed in to see him in his study one night, worried by a news item in one of the evening papers which had been discussed at breakfast that morning. 'I hope you don't think that I talked?' she said.

'I would trust you with my life,' he answered, 'and what is much more important, I would trust you with the future of our country.'

Number 10 now became overcrowded with the comings and goings of military staff and secretaries, so Lloyd George commandeered the garden and had huts put up. Out of the windows of the Cabinet Room, the ministers could now see neat rows of large garden sheds, which came to be known as the Garden Suburb.

When General, later Field Marshal, Sir William Robertson, Chief of the Imperial General Staff, once called early in the morning to keep an appointment with the Prime Minister, he was kept waiting in Frances Stevenson's office which adjoined the Cabinet Room. Frances tried to keep him happy but his impatience grew after a while and he flung open the Cabinet Room doors, expecting to face Lloyd George. Instead he was set upon by a large Chow dog who stood on his back legs to lick his face. Frances explained that it was the Prime Minister's pet and that it slept in the Cabinet Room. The Prime Minister would now see him upstairs in his study.

Robertson had come to discuss General Sir Douglas Haig, Commander-in-Chief of the British forces in France. Lloyd George held the view that Haig was an incompetent bungler and must be replaced. 'I can't get rid of 'im,' said the horrified Robertson in the plebeian accent he never lost. ''E's 'ighly thought of and 'ighly connected. The man's a personal friend of 'is Majesty,' he complained.

Lloyd George sympathized with his situation but pointed out that he had to stop thinking small. Robertson was the only man in British history to rise from private to general and just because Haig was a gentleman, Sandhurst, and all that regimental-silver-in-the-Mess twaddle, it didn't mean he had to be saluted. 'I'm a peasant too,' he pointed out, 'and I'd as soon kick him up his well padded arse as look at him!'

Robertson, a loyal military man, protested that Haig was a damn good

Sir Douglas Haig, Commander-in-Chief of the British forces in France in the First World War. Lloyd George regarded Haig's strategy with horror and accused him of using the bodies of the dead as bridges for the living

Sir William Robertson, Chief of the Imperial Staff during the First World War. Robertson was the only man in British military history to rise from the rank of private to that of field marshal

soldier, which infuriated the Prime Minister. 'He couldn't command a girls' hockey team. He's left a million of our youth, the seed corn of the nation, hanging rotting on the wire out there, or sprawled in the cowshit of Flanders. We are losing this war. I want a unified allied command and I want the best Supreme Commander available, regardless of nationality!'

The running of Number 10 was naturally left to Margaret, who coped admirably with the endless stream of callers and visitors. When journalists came round with legitimate excuses for securing interviews, she was always wary of the possible gossip columnists among them and put on a brave enough face to ward off any suspicions they might have about the Prime Minister and his pretty secretary.

When asked if she thought it a strain being the wife of the man who carried the responsibility of the war on his back, she answered, 'If you mean, do I worry about him, yes I do. But he's the one who carries the burden and he never shows it to me. To me he's as carefree and loving and light hearted as if he hadn't a worry in the world. He's the best husband a woman could wish for.'

But on returning from France, after visiting the Front, it was to Frances Stevenson that Lloyd George turned for love and affection. The arrangement of having his dutiful mistress wherever he wanted her suited him well, even if the situation was by no means all roses for her. They had many petty arguments, usually on the theme of divorce and marriage. She needled him by suggesting that she might go off and marry a millionaire, and he needled her by claiming that this would suit him even better. With her respectably married no one would suspect anything. War had taught him the value of camouflage, at least!

Appearances was the 'cross' that Frances had to bear throughout the relationship. When certain people and certain newspapers began noticing them together Lloyd George was quite ruthless with her, stopping her from riding in his official car, not requesting that she should no longer do so, but ordering her not to.

One day, however, Frances rebelled and Margaret entered the panelled dining room to find one of the servants altering the place cards she had set out for an official dinner that evening. Surprised, she asked him what he was doing, only to learn that the Prime Minister's secretary had asked him to put the guests in different places to provide a 'better mix'. Needless to say the butler was ordered immediately to put them back as they were.

After one of their many tiffs, when Frances protested in despair that she was always pushed in the background and had to put up with all his hypocrisy rising out of their discretion, Lloyd George told her that Margaret and the family were going to Wales for several weeks. He therefore invited her to stay with him at Number 10, instead of his having to visit her at the apartment he had given her in Chester Square. It was something for her to look forward to, and with the war naturally being her lover's first pre-occupation, between stolen kisses behind closed Cabinet doors, she again took a back seat while waiting for the time when she would have him all to herself.

The Admiralty was now giving Lloyd George headaches and he summoned to Number 10 Sir Edward Carson, First Lord of the Admiralty, together with two admirals, to work out a better naval strategy. With them they brought a young statistician to prove to the Prime Minister that the Royal Navy was whipping the German Navy off the High Seas and keeping it cowering in harbour. But Lloyd George was not interested in the German Navy, he was concerned about the British merchant ships which were being relentlessly attacked by German submarines. 'If the Huns' submarines keep sinking half a million tons a month of our merchant shipping, as they did last month, how long will it be before we starve to death?' he asked the statistician. 'Down to subsistence level within three months, Sir,' came back the answer.

The Royal Navy might have three thousand fighting vessels, but this did not impress Lloyd George. 'They're sitting on their backsides in port, manicuring their decks, while the German crocodiles are dragging our merchantmen under!'

The outcome of the row which ensued was that Lloyd George had the Merchant Navy organized into convoys flanked by Royal Navy destroyers whenever they sailed long distances. This move cut the shipping losses by ninety per cent, a personal victory that made the headlines in the papers – and added a few more 'top' people to the lengthening list of those who bitterly resented Mr Lloyd George's impertinence.

As soon as Margaret had left for Wales, Lloyd George and Frances leapt into each other's arms, though they remained, on the face of it, discreet. Turning up late in the evening, Frances Stevenson would tell the policeman on duty outside Number 10 that she was working late: 'The French have called an unexpected conference in Paris,' or, 'We have to do our homework.'

Taking all the necessary precautions not to arouse the domestic staff's suspicions, she would go through an elaborate charade in her office and in the Prime Minister's study before joining him upstairs in his bedroom. There, sharing a bottle of Irish whiskey in bed they would tell each other jokes, gossip, or sometimes talk very seriously for, after making love, Lloyd George could sometimes be morose.

One night he turned to her and said, 'I'm going to ask you a very terrible thing, Frances *cariad*. When I go, and I *will* go first, our ages will see to that – I want you to come with me. Don't ask me to explain. Yes, I'm a pagan, I've always been a pagan, despite all the hymn singing. But I just know if we went together there'd be something in the power of love. . .our rare love. . . .'

This strange morbid declaration gave Frances confidence and she slowly started busying herself more with the domestic side of his life than was wise, going so far as to ask one of the servants to help her change round the paintings in the drawing room once Margaret had returned.

Mrs Lloyd George interrupted the hanging and asked her what she thought she was doing. Embarrassed, the Prime Minister's private secretary explained that she thought the new arrangement would suit the decor better. She made a great *faux pas*, not only suggesting that they would look better, but that Lloyd George had shown a taste for these different pictures when choosing the decor for himself elsewhere.

Producing a scarf belonging to Frances, Margaret handed it over with a freezing smile. 'I found this on the main landing by the bedroom. I believe I've seen you wearing it.'

Frances immediately realized that her lover's wife knew perfectly well what had been going on in her absence. She managed to put a brave face on the incident, but Margaret had not finished with her. 'We'll leave the pictures as they were, I think,' she started. 'You have a demanding position, private secretary to a Prime Minister, people courting you in the hope you'll be able to influence him on their behalf, protecting him from nuisances he doesn't want to see, sharing his . . . thinking . . . on great matters of State. I know I'm just a country mouse, but I do understand more than you think.'

This speech shook Frances enough for her to run straight to Lloyd George and tell him that their affair had been discovered. He hardly reacted at all. He had taken it for granted that his wife assumed he slept with his secretary. But Frances had not. What troubled her on top of it all was that they had now done so at Number 10.

'Fran, *cariad*, what's the difference – your flat or here?'

She accused him of having no conscience, and again he laughed at her, 'I know. It's one of my great strengths as a politician.'

Lloyd George had more than Frances to put up with, and she was by no means his main concern. He needed more munitions, 'a torrent of weapons pouring into the hands of our men', and the only man who could get them was Churchill, whom he wanted as his Minister of Munitions. Churchill, however, was even more unpopular than Lloyd George himself due to the bloody failure of the British and French naval expedition that Churchill had sent into the Dardanelles against the Turks in 1915, and Lloyd George had to fight everyone to get him.

He also wanted to get rid of Haig.

In a heated argument at Number 10 the Prime Minister accused him of using the bodies of the dead as bridges for the living. 'Do you know what you are called by your men? The Prince of Death!' Haig had personally lost half a million men taking a patch of Flanders the size of Regent's Park, and still he could only see them as numbers, tin soldiers to be knocked down in a game.

Lloyd George was later to explain to his horrified son, Richard, Haig's simplistic view of his strategy: 'Imagine a game of draughts. You have twelve pieces, your opponent has nine. You start exchanging pieces, men for men. When you've exchanged three you're half again as strong as he is – nine to six. When you've exchanged six you're *twice* as strong. You see, that's the theory. It's the arithmetic of power.'*

Lloyd George ended the meeting with Haig, realizing he could not communicate with such a fearfully blind mind. Within days he arranged with the French Prime Minister for Marshal Foch to be Supreme Commander of the Allied Armies in France, which put him over both Haig and the American commander, General Pershing.

On 10 November 1918, the terms of an armistice entailing the withdrawal of German forces to the east bank of the Rhine, the surrender of the High Seas Fleet and vast stocks of ammunition, were drawn up and presented to the Germans. On 11 November at 11.00 a.m. Germany surrendered and the Great War came at last to an end. That afternoon Lloyd George addressed the House of Commons and later, accompanied by Margaret and Megan, drove to the country for a rest. 'I am feeling today like a man who has been in a big thing that is over. He is at a loose end, he does not know what to do. I feel like that,' he said, 'I have had a terrible time during the past four and a half years. We shall announce the election next week.'

On his return to Downing Street the following day he was cheered endlessly as 'The Man Who Had Won the War'. He was tired out, and not ready for the shock he was to receive a few days later. Crossing the entrance hall of Number 10 one morning, he found it full of suitcases, and Margaret dressed as though for a long journey.

'I'm going back to Wales,' she announced. 'We won't be seeing each other again, very much. You're a great man, Dai. You're probably the only man who could have won this war for us. I couldn't interfere with that. But you're also a selfish, blind, greedy, self-indulgent pig and there is nothing to keep me here now.'

The Prime Minister was shattered and protested, only to receive further reprimand:

For God's sake man, for once in your life listen! It may be important to you. For half a lifetime you've treated me on a level with our dogs. You may think you treated me with respect, but I consider you have been sly. You've never thrown it in my face, everyone has co-operated with you, turned a blind eye, treated me with deference and courtesy, but everyone has *known*! You made me hate London. You made me feel there was nothing I could do for you here. I spent a lot of time in Wales, because there I didn't have to see things, and there I could help you, but do you know what I've been doing in Wales all these years? I've been nursing your constituency. Do

* *Lloyd George*, by Earl Lloyd George, Frederick Muller, 1960.

you know what they called you in Caernarvon? The climber who pulled the ladder up behind him.

Lloyd George protested, tried to reason with her, make a point in his defence, but she had one more ace up her sleeve.

'Tell me,' she asked, 'did you ask *her* to die with you too? Oh David, what are we supposed to do, sit on your funeral pyre, holding hands?' And thus she swept out, leaving him with the realization, for the first time in his married life, that here was a woman of style.

In the general election in December the Lloyd George-Bonar Law coalition won an overwhelming victory, and the former was now left with the unenviable task of helping to rebuild Europe, together with Clemenceau of France, Orlando of Italy and Woodrow Wilson, the President of the United States, who all signed the Treaty of Versailles in June 1919, establishing the League of Nations.

But matters at home began to decline, and after the excitement of victory came the problems of unemployment and bitterness. Britain found that Lloyd George's promise of a land fit for heroes to live in was not to be.

At Number 10, with the war over, the Garden Suburb was removed and in the mornings Lloyd George happily played on the new lawn with his two granddaughters, Olwen's and Richard's children, then took them for long walks in St James's Park. When the Cabinet Room had been neatly prepared for a meeting, he would lift the girls up on the table and watch them step from clean blotting pad to clean blotting pad as though playing hop-scotch on paving stones, or even push them heartily down the length of the polished wood between carefully laid out places where Ministers of the Crown would soon be sitting.

In 1922 it was made clear by the Conservatives that Lloyd George had served his purpose in the coalition, and he handed in his resignation to the King. George V accepted it reluctantly, believing that he would soon be back as Prime Minister.

But once Lloyd George left Number 10 he never returned, though he managed to keep on living with his two women. Reconciled to the life they had established, Margaret and Frances shared their ex-Prime Minister. Margaret had the upper hand most of the time, Frances escaping by the back door of whichever house or apartment she was co-habiting when 'the wife' arrived.

In 1929 Frances gave birth to a daughter, Jennifer, who was clearly also Lloyd George's. But, despite the possible scandal, he continued his parliamentary life, helped more and more by Margaret who jealously guarded the Caernarvon borough seat and helped her daughter Megan to secure the Liberal nomination for Anglesey.

Moving day, October 1922. Lloyd George, the out-going Prime Minister, supervising the removal of his belongings from Number 10

Jennifer's birth was a psychological setback for Lloyd George and his relationship with Frances waned, leaving her vulnerable to the advances of Colonel Thomas Tweed, the head of Lloyd George's political office, with whom she had a sudden passionate affair. Margaret learned of this cladestine liaison from her maid and, not unnaturally, told her husband about it with some satisfaction.

Lloyd George, feeling betrayed, temporarily turned his back on Frances and became extremely grateful for the peace and comforting love Margaret was still able to provide. Together they went abroad, particularly enjoying a trip in the South of France in 1938 when they celebrated their golden wedding anniversary. At a special luncheon at the Carlton Hotel in Cannes, they were joined by Winston Churchill who gave them a silver loving cup from which everyone toasted their health. In a brief speech of thanks Lloyd George humorously paid tribute to his wife. 'Marriage is the greatest and oldest partnership in the world, the best and truest friendship, I need hardly

Reconciliation at Lloyd George's eightieth birthday party: his second wife, Frances, with Megan Lloyd George

say that my wife and I are of different temperaments. One is contentious, combative and stormy. That is my wife. Then there is the partner, placid, calm, peaceful and patient. That is me.

At the outbreak of the Second World War, Churchill asked Lloyd George to join the Cabinet but, now seventy-six, he declined, preferring to return to Wales.

In November 1940 Margaret, visiting neighbours in Criccieth, slipped on a highly polished parquet floor, a painful but minor accident. X-rays, however, revealed she had cracked her hip bone. Though she was seventy-five and had to take to her bed, she did not think it was anything to worry about. But after two months the crack showed no sign of healing and

179

Margaret became weak and feverish. Realizing that she was not fighting back, the family became very concerned and contacted Lloyd George who happened to be in London. He returned immediately with the King's doctor, Lord Dawson of Penn, but due to a snowstorm they got marooned in a village some distance away.

On that morning, 20 January, Margaret died. Lloyd George heard the dreadful news over the telephone and from that moment, friends said, he himself became visibly older, weaker and lost his characteristic spark of life.

Alone, he returned to Frances with whom he had become reconciled. She had broken with Tweed, the love affair was forgotten and, having promised, thirty-eight years earlier, that when he was free to do so he would marry her, Lloyd George kept his word. In 1943, two years after Margaret's death, they became man and wife, causing a rupture with his sons and daughters who held their mother's memory too highly not to feel it had been violated.

Lloyd George and Frances went to live in Churt, Surrey, and in January 1945 he became Earl Lloyd George of Dwyfor and Viscount Gwynned. But only a month later, his mind, curiously dominated by religion, began to wander. 'The sign of the cross,' he was heard to murmur in a half sleep. 'You have to hand it to the Catholics,' he'd exclaim *à propos* of nothing. 'Papal sweets!' he said out loud once or twice.

He slept a good deal, then one day he asked Frances if she had made the necessary arrangements with 'those Caernarvon people', meaning the undertakers. On 20 March he grew very weak, hardly spoke at all but beamed happily at those who came to see him. Six days later, with Frances holding one hand and Megan the other, he died quietly.

'We have lost our most distinguished member,' Aneurin Bevan said a few days later, 'and we have lost the most iridescent figure that ever illuminated the British political scene.'

He was buried at Llanystumdwy in Wales.

CHAPTER SEVEN

Underdog

James Ramsay MacDonald was Prime Minister of Britain's first Labour Government, which came to power in January 1924.

Born in 1866 in Lossiemouth, a fishing village on the banks of Moray Firth, he was the illegitimate son of John MacDonald, a ploughman, and Anne Ramsay, a farm housekeeper. He was brought up in his grandmother's home, a two-roomed hovel with a thatched roof backing onto the railway line. It was a place of dire poverty.

He went to the local school and fortunately made friends with an elderly neighbour, an avid reader, who encouraged him to make use of his small collection of books which contained, among other masterpieces, the complete works of Shakespeare and Dickens. Little James read every page.

At twelve he was due to leave school to go to sea and become a fisherman, like the majority of Lossiemouth lads. But his headmaster, regarding him as his brightest pupil, reduced his fees so that he could stay on and become a pupil-teacher, thus ensuring that a bright mind would not be lost like so many others.

Though from the beginning James had had to endure poverty, he refused to accept that it was inevitable. Preferring scientific subjects to the classics, he took nothing for granted but examined everything and, at sixteen, made a study of the economic situation around him which was keeping him where he was. He soon realized that wealth was unfairly distributed and so started taking an interest in politics.

He became involved in a local election, supporting the local Radical candidate; the Labour Party was not yet in existence. He did not make speeches, but helped in whatever way he could to organize the campaign, and soon gained the reputation of being a young man with ideas.

His beliefs – that all was not as it should be – were strengthened by a book published at the time, *Progress and Poverty* by Henry George, which

181

Ramsay MacDonald's childhood home in Allan Lane, Lossiemouth

familiarized people with the idea of common use of property, of common creation of values, of common claims to share in aggregate wealth, and led them to discuss the problems of poverty, not as a result of personal short-comings, but as an aspect of a certain form of social organization.

It confirmed James's own thoughts that direct experience was the truth and that the artist's imagination, not the statistician's, could show him the way out, though there could be no short cut. He knew there was only a long uphill road of continuous effort ahead, lit fleetingly by glimmers of hope, but he set out, leaving Lossiemouth to take up an appointment as assistant to a clergyman who was running a boys' club in Bristol.

Once there he joined the Social Democratic Federation, where he made his first political speech, addressing an audience of three. He then discovered that his employer's ideals on social reform were not his own, so returned to Scotland.

After a while he was offered another appointment connected with the Church, this time in London, and with a shilling in his pocket he set off for the great capital, only to discover on his arrival that the job did not exist.

He was eighteen, stranded, on the point of starvation, but was determined not to go back to Lossiemouth. Like the majority of the unemployed he wandered for days around the streets of London looking for work and was amazed and appalled at the abundant wealth contrasting with the fearful poverty. It made him more determined than ever to change society.

Eventually he found employment addressing envelopes for a newly formed cyclist touring club. This led to another job as an invoice clerk in a warehouse which paid for a bed but no midday meal, so he spent his lunch hour at the Guildhall Library in the City, and his evenings studying at

Birkbeck College, where he took a correspondence course in science, aiming to take a Queen's Scholarship. Working all day and studying until two or three in the morning took its toll, and inevitably he collapsed one day. It was bad timing, for he was too sick to take the exams he had worked for and, depressed, he abandoned the idea of a scientific career.

In November 1887 he joined a meeting of Socialists in Trafalgar Square who were demonstrating in defiance of a proclamation prohibiting processions or meetings in that very place. Fighting broke out between the demonstrators and the police and a number of people were injured. Referring to the incident, James later wrote: 'These troubles arose in connection with an agitation of the unemployed. Trade was very bad and men out of employment were being told for the first time in their lives that they ought to starve in private. They were told to come out in their rags and they came, the just with the unjust, and as usual those who looked on saw only the unjust.

At this demonstration he met Thomas Lough, the Gladstonian Liberal candidate for West Islington, who was looking for a private secretary. When the politician learnt that young James had studied economics, had helped in an election campaign in Scotland and had ideas about government, he engaged him immediately at a salary of £75 per annum. 'Now I have attained fortune,' James Ramsay MacDonald wrote to a friend. He stayed with Lough for four years, during which time he immersed himself totally in the workings of the political scene.

In 1893 he joined the Fabian Society, a middle-class political body meeting in each other's comfortable drawing rooms, named after Quintus Fabius Maximus who was nicknamed Fabius the Delayer because he achieved success over Hannibal by refusing to give direct battle. It was a movement of brilliant intellectuals, chief among whom were Sidney and Beatrice Webb, H. G. Wells, George Bernard Shaw, Graham Wallis, Sidney Oliver and Edward Pease. It was basically a research institution furnishing information for social reform. As a Fabian and with his experience as secretary to a prominent Liberal, MacDonald began to sell articles to newspapers. He became a staff journalist on the *Weekly Dispatch*, then the *Echo*, a London evening paper, and then the *Daily Chronicle*, earning extra money as a freelance.

Following the formation of the Labour Party by Keir Hardie, James Ramsay MacDonald became editor of the *Labour Leader*, his immediate task being to awaken the organized workers to the need for political action through continuous propaganda.

Energetic and committed, he also worked as secretary of the London Trades Council, which represented some two hundred societies and a hundred trades. It was the biggest and most powerful representative body of workers in London and he wanted the Trades Council and the Trades Union

Keir Hardie, founder of the British Labour Party

Congress to change their attitudes about standing aloof from politics in order to get their support for the new Labour Party.

In 1895, at twenty-nine, he stood as Independent Labour Party candidate at Southampton, giving an impressive election address.

The Principles and Programme upon which I shall ask your opinion on the day of the election can be briefly stated. I ceased to trust in the Liberal Party when I was convinced that they were not prepared to go on and courageously face the bread and butter problems of poverty, stunted lives and pauper-and-criminal-making conditions of labour. Neither Tories nor Liberals have a Labour policy. Neither of them can answer why house rents are going up, why the struggling shopkeeper and wage earner are reaping so little benefit from the increasing size of the town, why the unemployment difficulty is becoming more pressing, what to do with machinery which is being introduced all round and which should make labour more easy but is, in reality, now beginning to take the place of labour. The monopolist owns the land and houses of Southampton, and keeps piling up a rent which he has never justly earned. I am, therefore, in favour of Land Nationalization; and as a step towards that end would begin at once by taxing, for local purposes, those extra values which your enterprise and the advantage of your natural position have created. I am also in favour of nationalizing the Railways, and Mining Royalties. I favour: An eight hour day. A drastic Employer's Liability bill with no contracting out. Reform of the Poor Law, including Old Age Pensions. Measures dealing with Unemployment, Direct Employment of Labour, Trade Union Conditions in Government Employment, and making Government, in fact, a Model Employer. Graduated Income Tax. Adult suffrage. Abolition of the House of Lords. Self Government for Ireland, Scotland, England and Wales. Payment of Election expenses and of Members. . . .

And so it went on, familiar now of course, but new and revolutionary then.

No one preaching Socialism as a practical and immediate political creed could hope to win. Ramsay MacDonald polled 886 votes, failed to get in, but was happy to learn that Keir Hardie and Thomas Burt had been elected.

While standing for Southampton he again fell ill, and this time had to go into hospital. While there he corresponded with Labour sympathizers and received many donations for the election fund. One of his strongest supporters was Margaret Gladstone (no relation of William Ewart Gladstone). with whom he started a regular exchange of letters. Eventually they met, and their established interest in politics was fired by an undeniable mutual attraction.

Their backgrounds were totally different. Margaret's father was a distinguished chemist and Professor of the Royal Institute, and her mother was the niece of Lord Kelvin, the highly respected inventor of electrometers, and a pure scientist.

The Gladstones were a typical middle-class family and on hearing of their daughter's association with a Socialist were very doubtful as to the wisdom of receiving him at all. Socialism was something one did not care to discuss in polite society.

Ramsay MacDonald with his wife Margaret and their eldest daughter, Ishbel, flanked by Andrew Fisher, a Socialist politician from Australia, and his wife

Although James Ramsay MacDonald impressed them by his sincerity and wide knowledge of political affairs, they could not help but dislike his Socialist activities and made this plain.

As some of the family were responsible for having started a mission in Notting Hill, Margaret had often helped, coming into contact with the very poor, and she had also worked for the Salvation Army. She had decided to dedicate her life to the Labour movement, so naturally her parents' attitude caused her some unhappiness.

She became engaged to James and they married in 1896, moving into a flat in Lincoln's Inn Fields. They then set out on a honeymoon to Canada, which they spent mostly in studying the political scene there. Though by no means rich, James's days of useless poverty were over and when they could afford it they travelled abroad, visiting Europe, the United States, South Africa and India, about which he wrote a book, *The Awakening of India*.

A pacifist, like Lloyd George, he opposed the Boer War and went against the tide of popular opinion. But in political circles the Ramsay MacDonalds were becoming known, and their social gatherings at their flat in Lincoln's Inn provided invaluable meetings for left-wing sympathizers.

In 1906 there was a general election. The Labour Party, which had only four members in the outgoing House of Commons, put fifty candidates into the field. Twenty-nine were returned; one was Ramsay MacDonald, new Member of Parliament for Leicester.

The Labour Party now had national recognition and during the next five years, the new members concentrated on consolidating their hard-won positions. By 1911, both James and Margaret were beginning to see the fruits of their endeavours ripen, but a series of terrible tragedies hit them. First, their youngest son, David, died of diphtheria. The following week James's mother died – he had set her up in her own little house in Loss-iemouth. A very dear friend of Margaret's also died, and she then became seriously ill with a form of blood poisoning.

'I am not ill,' she protested. 'Only tired.' By now the couple had had six children, three boys and three girls, the last of whom was only a few months old. Margaret was more than tired, her son's death had drained her of energy. Her condition worsened rapidly and, in September 1911, she died.

James was shattered. Going through the motions of living, he carried on because he had to, moving from Lincoln's Inn to a house in Hampstead where he hired the services of a Dutch housekeeper to look after the children who were too young to go to a boarding school, the others being educated by funds Margaret thankfully had left for that purpose.

A lonely man who had shared his political life with his wife, he knew he would never be able to forget her, or indeed be totally happy ever again. Alone he carried on, immersing himself more than ever in the political scene.

In 1914 he opposed the war, believing that Britain was morally wrong to get involved. Speaking in his constituency, he declared that he did not think war was necessary, he thought it was very rarely necessary, and that when necessary it was rarely successful.

There was an outcry and the publication of his speech was a foretaste of the persecution to come. Exchanges of letters in *The Times* and articles in the press deliberately misinterpreted his statements and in his defence he wrote an article in the *Labour Leader*, which was also printed as a broadsheet attacking the Foreign Minister, Sir Edward Grey:

When Sir Edward Grey failed to secure peace between Germany and Russia, he

The Labour Party on the terrace of the House of Commons in 1906. At the General Election they had fielded fifty candidates, twenty-nine of whom were returned. Among these were, seated, James Ramsay MacDonald (third from left), Arthur Henderson (fourth from left), Keir Hardie (third from right), and Will Crooks (first right). Philip Snowden is standing at the back (eighth from right) and Will Thorne stands at the extreme right of the photograph

Ramsay MacDonald with two of his daughters in 1910

worked deliberately to involve us in the war, using Belgium as his chief excuse. I come back to the statement which I think I have clearly proven – that European war is the result of the existence of the Entente and Alliance, and that we are in it in consequence of Sir Edward Grey's policy. The Government supplied the idealism for this war by telling us that the independence of Belgium had to be vindicated. It was a pretty little game of hypocrisy, which the magnificent valour of the Belgians will enable the Government to hide up for the time being. Want is in our midst and Death walks with Want. And when we sit down and ask ourselves with the fullness of knowledge 'Why has this evil happened?' the only answer we can give is, because Sir Edward Grey has guided our foreign policy during the past eight years. So anxious was Germany to confine the limits of the war, the German Ambassador asked Sir Edward Grey to propose his own conditions of neutrality, and Sir Edward Grey declined to discuss the matter. This fact was suppressed by Sir Edward Grey and Mr Asquith in their speeches in Parliament.

Both withheld the full truth from us. Had this been told us by Sir Edward Grey, his speech could not have worked up a war sentiment. The hard, immovable fact was that Sir Edward Grey had so pledged the country's honour, without the country's knowledge, to fight for France or Russia that he was not in a position even to discuss neutrality.

James Ramsay MacDonald was labelled a traitor.

Misrepresented and scorned, his meetings broken up, he lost many friends who abandoned him because they were unable to support his views. No public man had so recently faced such unpopularity; he was regarded as propaganda for the Germans and wherever he went to speak, the occasion became an excuse for riots.

On 26 October 1914, the following resolution was adopted by his Leicester constituency:

That this meeting of the Executive Committee of Leicester Liberal Association desires to place on record its strong disapprobation of the attitude taken up by the senior member for Leicester–Mr Ramsay MacDonald–in regard to Sir Edward Grey; and deprecates the effects of his utterances and writings in encouraging the enemy, discouraging the response to our country's call, and creating a false impression in neutral States of Britain's art in diplomacy antecedent to the war, and feels compelled to entirely disassociate itself from his position of criticism and attack upon responsible Ministers of the Crown at this time of the country's supreme need.

A Labour supporter who had followed Ramsay MacDonald's career from its beginnings wrote to a newspaper:

Mr MacDonald alone outside Germany asks the world to wait for further evidence before the gentle, inoffensive innocent is convicted. Mr MacDonald must find another constituency. Personally, I should be glad if he would find another country. He is out of place in England. He cannot love England, or he would serve her. He neither serves nor encourages, he merely cavils.

From now on, whenever he tried to speak, he was shouted down, abused, and called a traitor. Horatio Bottomley, journalist, financier and founder of the jingoistic magazine *John Bull*, who had been stung by a reference in the *Labour Leader* to 'Horatio Bottomley, birthplace and parentage unknown' with which MacDonald had not actually been connected, published MacDonald's birth certificate prominently in an issue of *John Bull*, adding the label 'bastard' to that of traitor. 'Thank God my mother is dead,' he told a friend. 'For this surely would have killed her.'

By 1915, as the full horror of the war became gradually apparent, matters improved a little for him and when he spoke at the Trades Union Congress in Bristol, a Conservative paper admitted: 'Seldom, surely, can any speaker at Congress have had a warmer or more rousing reception than greeted Mr Ramsay MacDonald when he arose to address the assembly. His speech was greeted with fervid, almost frantic enthusiasm.'

And his address was a plea for unity in the ranks of the Labour Party.

He left for the Continent that year to serve his country in a Red Cross unit. He was forty-nine years old. No sooner had he set foot in Belgium than the authorities arrested him under instructions from the British, who considered him undesirable to be serving on the Western Front in any capacity. Lord Kitchener heard of the incident and was so shocked that he apologized to Ramsay MacDonald and immediately granted him a free pass to wherever he wished to go.

In 1918 came the end of the war and a new general election. MacDonald stood again for Leicester, but was beaten, and though for the next four years he continued on the fringe of politics, he also wrote, 'I have nothing to cherish but our memories.' In 1922, however, he was returned as member for Aberavon in Wales, and once more took the reins of power, becoming chairman and leader of the Labour Party and Leader of the Opposition.

Travelling daily from his Hampstead home to the House of Commons by bus or underground, he left all the household duties to his eldest daughter, Ishbel, who was now twenty years old. With one brother married and the other in Wales looking after constituency business, she took care of her two younger sisters who were still at school.

In October 1923 Bonar Law died and Stanley Baldwin took his place as Conservative Prime Minister. In December he went to the country seeking a mandate to introduce tariffs to protect British industry. The Conservatives were returned with an insufficient majority, and Labour became the larger of the two opposing parties.

One day, Ishbel, alone in Hampstead, was surprised to receive a personal note from Number 10 Downing Street. It was from Mrs Baldwin, suggesting she might like to come around and have a chat. She duly presented herself timidly at the historic house, only to be stopped and questioned by the policeman on duty outside the door, who asked her the nature of her business.

'My name is Ishbel MacDonald, I'm the eldest daughter of Mr Ramsay

MacDonald the Labour politician and Leader of the Opposition. Mrs Baldwin, the Prime Minister's wife, asked me to call.'

'I see, Miss,' said the officer, quite unimpressed. Fortunately Mrs Baldwin opened the door herself and welcomed her in. Quickly she explained that it was customary for Prime Ministers' wives, incoming and outgoing, to meet, and as she knew Mrs Ramsay MacDonald had died, thought the eldest daughter would probably be in charge. One could not expect the men to look after a house, they were too busy for one thing and didn't know anything about it anyway.

Ishbel protested that her father had not yet been made Prime Minister, that perhaps their meeting was a little premature, but Mrs Baldwin swept that idea aside. 'With unemployment, tariff barriers . . . Stanley's got it all wrong. The Conservatives will be defeated on a vote of No Confidence this afternoon and then the King will call upon your father. First Labour Government in history. Rather exciting! The boat trains to the Continent are already jammed with people stampeding abroad.'

Ishbel pointed out that her father was not a monster, which Mrs Baldwin thought quite funny, and they started a tour of the whole house.

Mrs Baldwin, a jolly woman, admitted to Ishbel that she would be pleased to go and was looking forward to long walks in the meadows and an occasional game of cricket, which she played quite often.

She then proceeded to tell Ishbel what furniture would remain and what would not. 'The sofas will be going, they're ours, and the easy chairs, the chaise longue. All the tables will be going, the carpets and the pictures. All the candlesticks and candelabra.'

In Baldwin's study everything would also be going, the desk, the chairs, the filing cabinets and so on. One little table would remain as it belonged to the Board of Works.

Ishbel soon realized that her father was going to be saddled with a vast residence but hardly any furniture, and doubted the sanity of accepting the honoured post of Premier.

James Ramsay MacDonald was duly called to Buckingham Palace and asked by George V to form an administration. He took office and moved into Number 10 Downing Street on 22 January 1924.

When father and daughter first entered the now very bare and empty house it was clear that the Board of Works, who were to supply any extra furniture the incoming Prime Minister might need, had thought fit to leave him a minimum of not very good quality pieces. There was not a stitch of linen, or one knife, fork or plate in the whole place. The State, it was clear, did not supply anything for private living, not even for official entertainment.

'There are forty rooms!' Ramsay MacDonald exclaimed, 'you could put our whole house into one of these reception caverns and it would still be

Ishbel MacDonald, who perforce became her father's housekeeper at Number 10 when he moved in in 1924

unfurnished. The January sales are on, get hold of your Aunt Bessie, get yourselves to the Co-op and buy whatever you think is needed in the way of crockery, linen and so on. But don't go mad!'

Ishbel then mentioned that such a house could not be run without domestic staff, whose salaries also had to come out of the Prime Minister's pocket. 'No wonder we've had three centuries of more or less Tory government,' her father said, 'nobody else can afford to do the job! How many will we need?'

She informed him that the Asquiths had had fourteen servants and the Baldwins ten, whereupon he decided that there would be major changes in tradition. Unlike former Prime Ministers, this one would have a parlour-maid instead of a butler, a cook, a pantrymaid and two chambermaids, five domestics in all, no more! He would also get the Board of Works to supply more furniture.

The formality of being Prime Minister, adapting to the new experiences of upper-class manners, was something with which the humble MacDonald knew he would have to cope. What he did not expect was that he would get help over the snobbery barrier from the King who, on their first meeting, was exceptionally understanding.

It's customary for the Leader of the House to send me a letter every night telling me what's gone on in the Commons that day. It is also usual to submit all important Foreign Office despatches to me before transmitting. And when my Ministers attend Court ceremonials, they are expected to wear Court dress. The full costs for such dress, I am told, can add up to seventy-three pounds, a monstrous amount, especially for men of little capital, so tell them that all I shall expect is evening dress and knee breeches which they can hire from Moss Brothers for tuppence ha'penny!

Ramsay MacDonald then submitted the names of the men he wanted in his Cabinet and the King pointedly remarked on their former positions in life: J. H. Thomas, Colonial Secretary, an engine driver; J. R. Clynes, Lord Privy Seal, a mill hand; Philip Snowden, Chancellor of the Exchequer, a factory worker. The new Government promised to be a major experiment in levelling down class consciousness.

The new home routine to which the MacDonald family now settled was unfamiliar to the girls and very much geared to what they could afford. The younger girls, in their green uniforms, walked to school in Camden Town to save bus fares. Instead of eating in their own, unheated, private part of the house, the family used the official dining room, which was heated by the State.

When a bill for groceries came from the Co-op – the sight of the van itself drawing up outside Number 10 to make deliveries was noted by the press – MacDonald had to warn his housekeeper daughter to be thriftier, for she had spent more on a day's purchases than he had earned in the same period of time, and as far as he was concerned, he was only there on sufferance. Should he lose the Liberal support, his Government would be out, and so would they all.

Though Ishbel worked very hard and adapted herself to the demanding conditions, she was aware that she could not replace her mother in her father's heart. He was always thinking of Margaret, mentioning her, referring to her, though she had now been dead fourteen years. It was a cross they all had to bear.

When she asked him if she or her sisters would ever be able to make him happier, he answered, 'Darling child, of course. You do, only in a different way. A man and a wife such as we were . . . walking the hills of Lossiemouth, she would say "Don't let's speak, let's walk silently, for then we speak most truly" . . . She was . . . rare. She believed in the absolute oneness of mankind. Sometimes I feel like a lone dog lost in the desert, howling for pain of the heart.'

There was an element of the ridiculous as the new Government settled in. None of the Cabinet members was used to the luxurious surroundings, or indeed the trappings that went with their unfamiliar positions of power. Most of them arrived late for the first meeting, blaming London Transport, for the buses were full and the nearest tube station was Westminster, quite a walk, especially for the Chancellor who was partially crippled. They were also not sure of how they should address MacDonald, nor each other.

'I've been doing some research into that,' the Premier told them. 'You call me Prime Minister, I call you by your surname or your office.'

Which some of them thought was a lot of damned rigmarole.

Rigmarole has its place [he defended]. It shapes the mind. Up to now Labour has used Parliament as a kind of Speaker's Corner – a soapbox of propaganda – aimed largely at people who already believe in us anyway. Now we have the chance to show that we're government timber, not just wreckers. We've got to be statesmen, not jumped-up hecklers. We must try to get world trade moving again, stop the French bleeding the Germans white in war reparations. If the Transport workers strike we must get volunteer drivers out on the roads while we negotiate. We do what has to be done. We govern!

Snowden criticized such an attitude, suggesting he was on a par with Baldwin and Asquith. Had he forgotten the MacDonald of the past, the boy from Lossiemouth?

MacDonald of Lossiemouth had not, 'I'm still your man,' he said. 'Bastard son of an itinerant cowman and a serving maid. Born and bred in a two-roomed shack next to stables, with six inch cracks between the walls to let in

Two members of Ramsay MacDonald's first Labour Cabinet, cruelly satirized by Low: Philip Snowden, who became Chancellor of the Exchequer; and J. H. Thomas, who was appointed Colonial Secretary

the stink of horse shit and horse piss!' He still carried a copy of his birth certificate in case he should ever forget who he was.

When General Sir Borlass Childs of the Special Branch of Scotland Yard reported to the new Prime Minister, MacDonald felt the full antagonism there was towards him and his Government from the Tory-orientated establishment. Childs informed the Premier that it was customary for his department to issue him with a weekly report concerning the revolutionary movements in the country, and he wanted to know whether MacDonald wanted the practice to continue.

The Prime Minister said he would, but asked why the revolutionary movements he had so far noted in the weekly reports were all Communist, ironically recommending that the reports might be a deal livelier from now on, and more comprehensive, if they also covered the activities of other political movements of an extreme nature – like the right wing? A little knowledge of the Fascist movement and its apostles might give an exhilarating flavour to the document, he suggested, and by enlarging its scope convert it into a complete work of art.

Ishbel also felt the draught of the conservative-minded establishment in the shape of the man from the Board of Works, with whom she had to deal concerning household effects. A snob, he looked down his nose at her and was so deliberately unhelpful that she had to tackle him as though she were his superior, not so easy for a twenty-year-old girl who considered herself from a humble background.

When the man complained that he had expected to be seen by the Prime Minister himself, she told him she was Mr Macdonald's political hostess:

I am also his social secretary, I am also his daughter. I have little knowledge of the world, but I do know this: the furnishings in this house are a disgrace! The Prime Minister is not prepared to accept the mean surroundings you seem to wish to impose on him. It doesn't matter that you've seen fit to put his office next to the Cabinet Room lavatory – I'm of no consequence – but my father is. He wants beautiful pieces, not stock room throw-outs. He wants good carpets. You are to borrow pictures from the National Gallery to put on his walls. You are to make the house fit for the first man of the land!

The man from the Board of Works, sneering, mentioned that he had understood they were Socialists, whereupon young Ishbel erupted, 'If you don't understand that it's to honour the office not the man, you understand nothing!'

Despite her efforts the rooms remained bleak and dowdy, and this nearly led to MacDonald's downfall, through an old friend who could not bear to see the Prime Minister live in such poor looking surroundings.

Alexander Grant was a wealthy Scottish biscuit manufacturer whose background was very similar to MacDonald's, coming from the humblest

circumstances and brought up in Morayshire, not far from Lossiemouth. Shocked one day at seeing MacDonald carrying his own suitcase and coming from the tube station, he insisted on giving him the loan of a Daimler car plus thirty thousand shares in his biscuit firm, McVitie & Price, the income from which would enable the impoverished Prime Minister to keep the car on the road with a chauffeur.

A while later, in no way connected with the generous gift, Grant brought up the question of a knighthood. It was not so much for himself, he argued, as for his wife who was rising in society and whom it would make so happy to have 'Lady' in front of her name. Grant was awarded a baronetcy in the next honours list, and MacDonald thought no more about it until a story appeared in the *Daily Mail*, virtually accusing him of taking bribes, having accepted a car, a chauffeur and £40,000 in exchange for granting the honour.

The news spread fast, and at the next Cabinet meeting J. H. Thomas accused MacDonald of wrecking the Party. 'You've gone down into the trough. You've soiled everything you've done for the character of the party. You had us looking like a Party of Government – with status, command,

It's Your **MONEY** He Wants

A Unionist poster for the general election of 1924, warning the British voter of the perils of voting for the Socialists, who were about to give a loan to Russia

authority. And now you've been caught with your hand in the till like a sneak thief!'

In his defence, MacDonald let it be known that Grant's father and his own uncle had both been guards on the Highlands Railway, and that was how far back the friendship went. For years Grant had been a regular visitor to their house, but apart from that, he had donated over £100,000 towards founding a Scottish National Library and it was for this magnificent contribution and other generous benefactions, such as schools and orphanages, that he had been honoured.

The damage, however, had been done, and a Labour Prime Minister could not afford such a scandal. He weathered the storm but it was a black mark against him and there was worse to come.

One of his first acts in power had been to recognize Soviet Russia. Now he wanted to lend Russia money – forty million pounds – so that the country could recover from the aftermath of the Revolution, and to lend to Germany too, so that she could recover from the war. His argument was simple. Both nations were bankrupt and bankrupt nations could not get prosperous again without help. If they were not prosperous they could not buy Britain's goods, if they could not buy Britain's goods unemployment could not be reduced.

Britain, however, was in the grip of a Communist phobia. People were seeing Reds round every corner and in an edition of *Workers' Weekly*, the organ of the Communist Party, the front page blazed out with 'Soldiers of the British Army! Let it be known that neither in the class war nor in a military war will you turn your guns on your fellow workers!'

Sir Patrick Hastings, the Attorney General, immediately decided the piece was an incitement to mutiny and a warrant was issued for the arrest of the editor, John Campbell. The Tories instantly capitalized on this and started telling the country that the article represented Labour Party policy.

Campbell was a man who had had both feet blown off in Flanders fighting for his country, he had been mentioned in despatches three times and then decorated for courage and bravery of an exceptional nature; furthermore, he was only the temporary editor and not in charge when the article was cleared for publication.

Because of these facts MacDonald managed to convince Sir Patrick Hastings that a prosecution would not succeed, but as Snowden pointed out, though they knew the truth, would it suit the Opposition to recognize it? MacDonald had quashed the case against a Communist agent who incited the forces to mutiny. It was a whitewash. He also wanted to loan Russia money, and he had been against the war . . . it all sounded very much of a piece.

However much MacDonald protested, the members of his Cabinet were desperately worried that he was being labelled a Red, and that the electorate thought he had the brimstone whiff of revolution about him:

Revolution! [MacDonald shouted] No one knows what the word means! I was in Europe in 1919, in the middle of it. I saw the prophets, the beautiful visionaries in action. Standing on tables howling and being howled at, provoking and being provoked! They went down to their graves, butchered, encompassed in hate and passion and chaos and what came after was worse than what had gone before. Don't talk to me of revolution. Revolution is the old enemy that makes me sweat in the hour before dawn.

When that particular storm was past and he thought he had overcome yet another crisis, MacDonald made a mistake in the Commons. Talking about it to Ishbel afterwards, he simply told her that he had 'bungled it'. 'I was asked by Kingsley Wood about the John Campbell affair. I meant to say I had exerted no pressure to have the prosecution dropped, that I'd simply uncovered the facts. Instead, I said I'd had nothing to do with it whatsoever.'

Ishbel did not understand why he thought it so dreadful.

'It was a lie, Ishbel. I was so angry at the way Wood put the question –

James Ramsay MacDonald (Ian Richardson) standing on the steps of Number 10 with his three daughters, Sheila (Jane Forster) Ishbel (Emma Piper), and Joan (Marion Owen Smith)

Ramsay MacDonald (Ian Richardson) with the wealthy biscuit manufacturer Alexander Grant (Robert Urquhart). MacDonald's grant of a title to Grant was to bring him untold trouble

Ramsay MacDonald (Ian Richardson)

implying that I was covering up for a fellow Bolshevik – that I just wanted to smash him. And I went too far. They'll concoct their story now. They'll link it up in some way with the Russian treaty and the forty million pound Russian loan and paint a picture that will bring me down. The Tories are already drawing up a motion of censure on the Campbell affair and the Liberals are with them. I'm done for.'

And he was right.

The Tories were already preparing for an election. A sympathetic print worker had sent him proof copies of the Tories' campaign leaflets, and they were as damning as they were false.

One claimed that 'A Vote for Socialism is a Vote for Communism'. Another showed Russian bogeymen in fur hats and ragged fur coats with the caption, 'We Come to Get You!', while a third showed a British overalled workman speaking the words, 'I Want Work' next to a Russian saying, 'I Wantski £40,000,000!' Another stated, 'Communism destroys Marriage' and warned against Labour Youth Clubs and Sunday Schools where children were baptised into the Communist faith and taught the principles of street fighting. Voters were warned that health visitors could be Communist spies and that if the Communists came to power, children would be taken away from their parents and become the property of the State.

MacDonald decided to call a general election. Labour seemed to be doing better than anyone had dared hope. Then, three days before polling day, the papers published a damning letter purporting to be from the Russian Communist leader, Gregory Zinoviev, to the British Communist Party, advocating preparations for armed revolution.

The Government had no time to prove it was a forgery. MacDonald realized that honesty of purpose was not all a man needed if that man was Prime Minister. He also needed guile, mendacity and deceit. MacDonald and his Party were overwhelmingly defeated and Baldwin came back, leading the Conservatives.

Ishbel invited Mrs Baldwin to visit her, as she had been invited. The women at least were friends, even if the behind-the-scenes political fighting had been less than Mrs Baldwin's beloved cricket. Ramsay MacDonald and his family left Number 10 and returned to Hampstead.

For five years he led the Parliamentary Labour Party during the 'Long Parliament', which was a dull affair. Then in 1929 he stood for Seaham in Durham, won a majority vote of 27,794, and Labour was returned to become the largest party in the House. He was again Prime Minister.

Older now and knowing the ropes, Ishbel managed the running of Number 10, again weathering the housekeeping storms. Meanwhile her father faced the grim economic crisis caused by two and a half million unemployed and the Government having insufficient funds to pay out unemployment benefit. In 1931 he offered to resign but was persuaded by

Ramsay MacDonald, the poor Scottish lad turned English country gentleman, with his daughter Joan at Chequers in 1924

the King to see the country through the crisis. He continued as Prime Minister, heading a National Government which included the Conservative and Liberal leaders, but only a small element in his own Party.

Ramsay MacDonald soldiered on for four more years, but eventually the sheer strain of the job, his continued loneliness without Margaret and the slow loss of his sight and brainpower forced him to resign.

He was appointed Lord President of the Council, fought again for the Seaham seat, but was defeated by Emmanuel Shinwell. He carried on trying to get back into the Commons, however, and in January 1936 he was returned as Member of Parliament in the Scottish Universities' by-election.

But he was ageing, and was regarded by many as a tired, ill and pathetic figure. He had, in earlier years, been vain about his appearance, and his imagination had been kindled by the magnificence of ceremonial tradition. Bernard Shaw once described him as 'a Highlander of the seventeenth century who had little in common with trade union leaders' and certainly a sentimental love affair with Edith, Marchioness of Londonderry, late in his life alienated some of his former Socialist colleagues who accused him of succumbing to the allurements of aristocratic society.

In 1937 James Ramsay MacDonald embarked on a cruise to South America, but quite unexpectedly died on 9 November during the Atlantic crossing.

Epilogue

Watch an old building with anxious care, guard it as best you may, and, at any cost, from any influence of delapidation. Count its stones as you would jewels of a crown. Set watchers about it, as if at a gate of a besieged city; bind it together with irons when it loosens; stay it with timber when it declines. Do this tenderly and reverently and continually and many a generation will still be born and pass away beneath its shadow.

RUSKIN

For the clearest picture of the domestic life of Number 10 Downing Street, we must turn to one of the children who lived in the house and saw several generations of Prime Ministers pass through its front door, if not 'pass away beneath its shadow'. Violet Bonham Carter, née Violet Asquith, wrote in 1941, 'I think of the house, not as an historic monument, nor as an official residence, but as the beloved home in which I spent eight of the happiest and most unforgettable years of my life'.

She first visited it aged six, when her father took her to have lunch with Mr Gladstone. 'His eagle face and the lightning in his eyes are my most vivid memory of that visit. His daughter, fearing that we might not approach the house in a sufficiently reverent spirit whispered on the doorstep "Now remember that you are on holy ground!"'

Fifteen years later she entered the house again as the daughter of a new Prime Minister, and was awed by the fact that she was moving into rooms and using the furniture that had served Benjamin Disraeli, Sir Henry Campbell-Bannerman, and A. J. Balfour. She hoped that the historic portraits on the walls and up the stairs might look down on her and perhaps check any urge she might have to behave foolishly. A dull, full-length copy of Pitt the Younger's portrait over the mantelpiece in the dining room was one she would not easily forget. Showing Sir Charles Holroyd, Keeper of the National Gallery, over the house she pointed it out to him, adding apologetically, 'I fear we have no originals in this room – that is only a dreary copy', to which he replied, 'I painted it'.

She found a small out-of-the-way room in the house which inexplicably gave her the sense of being in the country. It was a sunny sitting room opening onto the garden, and when the family first moved in she chose it as her own. 'My father gave it to me and his Parliamentary Secretary, who had pegged out a pre-emptive claim to it, was so angry that he tore out the telephone by the roots, exclaiming "She shan't have this anyway!"'

The Parliamentary Secretary moved to a room which opened onto the lobby outside the Cabinet Room, where there was a bust of Wellington, a bookcase full of Hansards, a weather glass and a table which she remembered as being usually covered with the hats of the Cabinet Ministers. 'This lobby used to be a thrilling place to run into during the dispersal of a Cabinet meeting. When a tug of war over some major issue had been taking place one could make a pretty good guess from the faces of the departing stream of Ministers which of them had been on the winning side.'

The messengers, whom she regarded as her guides, philosophers and friends, also made a study of Cabinet Ministers as they helped them on with their coats, 'You'd never believe it Miss, but Mr X is the only Minister who uses a looking glass before he goes out!' might be one of their secret observations.

She remembered her father at work, sitting at a vast writing table near the window in the grandest of the four reception rooms on the first floor, when he did not mind being interrupted. When it was vital that he should not be disturbed, he took refuge in the Cabinet Room below.

After the Asquiths moved out, the house was occupied first by the Lloyd Georges, next by Bonar Law, who was Prime Minister for only just over six months, then by Ramsay MacDonald and Stanley Baldwin who were in and out between 1923 and 1937, the former twice, the latter three times, facing the abdication of King Edward VIII over his union with Mrs Simpson in 1936.

Neville Chamberlain was the next Prime Minister, but he and his wife did not move in immediately. On looking over the house they realized it would lack the privacy they desired, with the living quarters mixed up with the State rooms and the secretarial offices. Lloyd George had moved his 'Welsh Embassy' from Number 11 to Number 10 with little regard to how everyone managed to mix in with him, while Bonar Law was a modest man who had never overcome his surprise at becoming Prime Minister, and Ramsay MacDonald's life style had depended on the Board of Works.

Mrs Chamberlain, with her artistic flair, decided she would restore Number 10 to its former eighteenth-century elegance. She consulted Sir Philip Sassoon who was not only the Minister of Works and a man of great taste, but whose sister, the Marchioness of Cholmondeley, had married into the Walpole family, and was therefore steeped in prime ministerial history. With his help she established the residential quarters on the second floor, putting in a second staircase as the main one only went up to the first floor. Ceilings were raised, walls straightened, old attic windows removed and larger ones put in until, as Violet Bonham Carter wrote when visiting it after completion:

The most miraculous change in the Downing Street of today is the beautiful new staircase put in by Sir Philip Sassoon connecting the first floor with the top floor rooms. These in our day were poky attic rooms reached only by back stairs. They have been transformed into the perfect bedrooms flooded with sunshine now used by the Prime Minister and Mrs Chamberlain. They open on a broad corridor with the atmosphere of a country house.

Indeed, a room at the north-west corner overlooking Horse Guards' Parade was earmarked for Neville Chamberlain, while his wife took a room opposite with a spacious bathroom *en suite*. The former bedrooms on the first floor were put to use as offices and the big kitchen downstairs was modernized, with a service lift installed to take food up to the passage just outside the State Dining Room. The alterations took ten months to complete, during which time the family lived at Number 11, where Neville Chamberlain had already been in residence as Chancellor of the Exchequer.

Again with Sassoon's help, Mrs Chamberlain re-furnished the house with eighteenth-century settees and Regency sofas in the now white State Drawing Room, red-upholstered furniture which had belonged to Clive of India in the pink painted State Drawing Room, and more eighteenth-century pieces in the yellow drawing room overlooking the park. The corresponding colours today are white, blue and gold.

In 1939 King George VI and Queen Elizabeth came to dinner one night in March and sat with twenty other guests in the State Dining Rom. Only twice before in the century had sovereigns dined at Number 10: first when George V and Queen Mary had dined with the Asquiths in 1911; the second when George VI and Queen Elizabeth had dined with the Baldwins before he retired as Prime Minister.

The Chamberlains lived a quiet life, enjoying a walk together in St James's Park every morning, to the bridge and back, followed at a discreet distance by a detective. When Neville Chamberlain resigned as Prime Minister in favour of Winston Churchill in 1940, Churchill insisted that he should not move out immediately as he was far from well. Then, late in June, the Churchills moved into Number 10, with Mary, their youngest daughter. Randolph was in the services and Diana and Sarah were married.

Mrs Churchill made one major alteration in the way of life in Downing Street. She gave Mrs Chamberlain's room with bathroom to the Prime Minister and took Neville Chamberlain's room overlooking Horse Guards'

Parade for herself. This ensured that the new Prime Minister could work in bed all through the day and night if he wished without charging down various corridors when he wanted a wash. Mary was given two rooms at the other end of the house and Major John Churchill, Winston's brother and a widower, had a room next to hers.

Throughout the early days of the war, during the fall of Holland and Belgium, the retreat from Dunkirk and the fall of France, Churchill used Number 10 as his headquarters. He seldom got up before 8.00 a.m. but often worked till 2.00 or 3.00 in the morning. Because of this Mrs Kathleen Hill, his secretary, and two assistants lived in, working in shifts to keep up with him. They would enter his bedroom with pad and pencil to find him propped up against a mountain of pillows after his breakfast and first cigar, and could tell immediately by the state of the newspapers by his side what they might be in for. If they lay beautifully folded on the counterpane, all was well. If they were crumpled in balls and hurled into various corners of the room, things augured badly.

Churchill dictated most of his speeches from his bed and it was in this room that Mrs Hill took down his historic speech following the Battle of Britain, 'Never in the field of human conflict. . . .'. He often dictated his speeches between bed and bathroom. The first draft then had to be typed out so that he could study and correct it and, more often than not, it was handed to him between bathroom and bedroom when he was wrapped only in a towel, or sometimes not even that.

When the Blitz started in September, he was urged to move into a special flat prepared for him in the Annexe at Storey's Gate, across the Foreign Office courtyard, facing St James's Park, but he hardly ever used it. He always insisted, however, that his staff should go down to the shelter that had been constructed near the kitchen, alongside the Treasury building, where some thirty bunks were available should long stays prove necessary.

Winston Churchill much preferred to see the raids through in the staff dining room, which was under the Cabinet Room. During the early days of the war he gave a number of intimate dinners there with a few friends, and wrote about one such occasion:

We were dining in the garden room when the usual night raid began. The steel shutters had been closed. Several loud explosions occurred around us at no great distance, and presently a bomb fell, perhaps a hundred yards away, on the Horse Guards' Parade, making a great deal of noise. Suddenly I had a providential impulse. The kitchen at Number 10 is lofty and spacious, and looks out through a large plate glass window about twenty-five feet high. The butler and parlour maid continued to serve the dinner with complete detachment, but I became acutely aware of this big window, behind which Mrs Landemare, the cook, and the kitchen maid, never turning a hair, were at work. I got up abruptly, went into the kitchen, told the butler to put the dinner on the hot plate in the dining room, and ordered the cook and the kitchen maid into the shelter, such as it was. I had been seated again at table only about three minutes when a really very loud crash, close at hand, and a violent shock showed that the house had been struck. My detective came into the room and said much damage had been done. The kitchen, the pantry, and the offices on the Treasury side were shattered.

We went into the kitchen to view the scene. The devastation was complete. The bomb had fallen fifty yards away on the Treasury, and the blast had smitten the large tidy kitchen, with all its bright saucepans and crockery, into a heap of black dust and rubble. The big plate glass window had been hurled in fragments and splinters across the room, and would, of course, have cut its occupants, if there had been any, to pieces. But my fortunate inspiration, which I might so easily have neglected, had come in the nick of time. As the raid continued and seemed to grow in intensity we put on our tin hats and went out to view the scene. Before doing so, however, I could not resist taking Mrs Landemare and the others from the shelter to see the kitchen. They were upset at the sight of the wreck, but principally on account of the general untidiness!

At the end of the war Number 10, like many other London houses, was in a bad state. Most of the walls were cracked, ceilings had come down or threatened to do so, and the window casings were peppered with pieces of shrapnel. It was battle scarred.

On 8 May 1945, the war with Germany ended; on 23 May Winston Churchill resigned and became head of a caretaker Government until the general election in July. Although he was immensely popular and regarded as the greatest war leader of all time, the electorate wanted a change, and he lost the election. Shaken by the result and stunned by the idea that the British people should dismiss him, he left Number 10 the same evening and moved to a suite at Claridges Hotel. He could not bear to remain one moment longer at Downing Street, where he had steered the country to peace.

Clement Attlee with his wife and four children were the next to occupy Number 10, but they could not move in immediately for much had to be done to make good the war damage. The Attlees took advantage of the presence of the builders to alter the house to suit the simpler way of life imposed by post-war restrictions.

Mrs Churchill, having lived on the second floor during the whole of the war without being able to carry out improvements, suggested that part of the floor should be converted into a self-contained flat. It took three months to complete the work, and when the Attlees eventually moved in, the Ministry of Works provided the furniture for the State rooms, while they brought in their own pieces for the private apartment.

Attlee liked the house enormously, particularly the privacy of the new quarters where nobody could intrude. He loved the stillness of the night there and the birds singing at the break of dawn. Like many other Prime Ministers he took to walking before breakfast in the park, and would have found it an ideal life, but for the occasional yet necessary official luncheons and dinners, of which he was always a little nervous.

He once told R. J. Minney the historian:

When we were entertaining members of the French Government, I had to pause and think for a moment, 'No, don't sit there, take this chair,' I said, for I felt it would be embarrassing for them to face the portrait of either Wellington or Nelson. With the Danes only Nelson was involved because he had bombarded Copenhagen. But they smiled as I placed them with their backs to the picture, and one of them said: 'We don't mind. It happened a long time ago.' When we entertained the Russians it was so much easier. I told them to sit anywhere they liked as they were not likely to find a Crimean General in that room.

In 1951 Winston Churchill was re-elected Prime Minister and moved back into Number 10. The Churchills did not go back to their war way of life, but used the old bedrooms on the first floor, next to the State rooms, for their personal use, leaving the Attlees' self-contained flat for their staff of private secretaries.

Churchill retired aged eighty in 1955 without fuss or fanfare because there was a newspaper strike. A last dinner was held at Number 10 for the Queen and Prince Philip, during which the elderly statesman remarked, after toasting Her Majesty, that he had drunk a similar toast to her great-great-grandmother when he was a cavalry subaltern some sixty years before.

Anthony Eden, Churchill's Chancellor of the Exchequer, was asked to take over and he immediately called a general election, winning with a comfortable majority. The Edens knew Number 10 well, for Clarissa Eden was Major John Churchill's daughter, and Winston's niece. She had plans to restore the main State rooms of the house to the style introduced by Walpole's architect more than two centuries before, but when estimates were discussed it became evident that with the credit squeeze the Treasury would never sanction such costs. But Sir Anthony did manage to introduce chandeliers in the Cabinet Room which up till then had been lit by three overhanging bowls.

The Edens lived at Number 10 for just under two years, during which time they entertained a great deal, mostly in a small breakfast room which they found more pleasant than the State Dining Room. They had seven servants living in, supplemented by outside caterers when necessary. With their wide range of personal friends the Edens were able to give small dinners with guests ranging from Dr Albert Schweizer to Greta Garbo. In addition they held official luncheons with Bulganin and Kruschev, Eisenhower, Foster Dulles, King Hussein of Jordan or King Feisal of Iraq.

In 1956, the Suez Crisis developed: British troops had left the Canal zone on 13 June and six weeks later Nasser seized the Canal. British and French forces were dropped by air near Port Said on 5 November, but the next day Eden announced that there would be a cease fire at midnight and that an international force would take over. In the House he said, 'As the dust settles it may well be that out of this anxiety a better opportunity will come than has ever been available before for the United Nations to prove itself a really effective international organization.' In January 1957 Sir Anthony Eden resigned due to ill health, to be succeeded by Harold Macmillan.

The Edens vacated Number 10 almost at once, taking the furniture they had brought with them. Harold Macmillan and Lady Dorothy, the daughter of the 9th Duke of Devonshire, were quite content to accept the house as it was, even with the Ministry of Works' replacement furniture. They lived a quiet life, entertaining only when officially necessary.

The state of the house was now, however, giving cause for concern. For some years Prime Ministers had been asked not to have more than a limited number of people in any of the upper rooms because the floors were weak and the old staircase had sunk a few inches. So a commission was appointed to report on the condition of Number 10 under the Earl of Crawford, an eminent figure in the world of art, a trustee of the National Gallery and the British Museum, Chairman of the National Trust, Royal Fine Arts Commission and National Art Collections Fund.

This commission reported that:

The sanitation and water supply were originally intended for a very limited use and have been constantly added to; the whole system is a complicated and makeshift arrangement. The pipe runs are faulty and the wiring needs renewal. When the Prime Minister is in residence a maintenance engineer has to be kept constantly available to attend to the lift in case of breakdown. The fire risk is abnormally high.

It recommended against demolition and replacement by an entirely new building, but suggested that, provided the work was undertaken before the structure suffered further deterioration, the house should be underpinned and strengthened, the roofs renovated, and the dried wood replaced.

The Macmillans agreed to move out in August 1960 to Admiralty House which became the temporary residence of the Prime Minister. The work of reconstruction, which began on 13 August, was entrusted to Raymond Erith, a man with a sensitive understanding of eighteenth-century buildings. It was estimated that the work would take two years but, due to a succession of strikes, it took three.

The fact that a large part of the house was used for twenty-four hours a day, seven days a week was taken into account when it was redesigned. Many of the office rooms were enlarged to cope with permanent staff, which during the war had overflowed into the Treasury together with their files, though some of these were stored in the basement next to the kitchen.

Erith added another storey to the house, running along the entire length of Numbers 10, 11 and 12, and a new lift was put in close to the front door. Throughout the house the old wooden floors were replaced by a double flooring of concrete encasing all the necessary water, heating and sanitation pipes, and electric and telephone wiring. When it was all completed, those who had known the house before found that Erith had completely managed to preserve Number 10's historical appearance and atmosphere. The entrance hall was unchanged, the corridor leading to the Cabinet Room, though almost completely reconstructed, did not seem visibly different, nor did the appearance of the Cabinet Room. The attractive ornamental cornices throughout were repaired and restored and even in the basement, despite many alterations, the famous kitchen was the same.

In 1963 Number 10 again became the official residence of the First Lord of the Treasury.

With over one hundred and thirty people working in the house, the overwhelming stillness and silence surprise the visitor entering Number 10 today. It is an unwritten rule that the staff use the main corridor only when absolutely necessary and that, with the exception of the Cabinet Ministers who tend to chatter loudly on leaving, everyone should talk quietly. The result is an atmosphere of cloistered calm.

All the staff use the front door unless exceptionally privileged, in which case they have a key to the garden gate opening out onto Horse Guards' Parade. A policeman is always on duty outside the front door and, inside the hall, a frock-coated doorkeeper sits in the dark green leather-hooded porter's chair, which dates back to Gladstone's time, waiting to let visitors in.

To the majority of tourists who stand outside Number 10 Downing Street staring at the familiar entrance, the house is yet another monument, but to Violet Bonham Carter, with whose words this book opened, it was a home where:

The pulse of great events [that] beats in every hour, Big Ben chiming close by, like a friend, in the silence of the night – a wood pigeon cooing in the may-tree in the gardens through a summer's afternoon – the Horse Guards' Parade alive with scarlet and trumpets as the Guards rehearse the Trooping the Colour on a May morning – the whiteness of the Treasury turning to silver in the twilight. These broken fragments are but part of it. Through them all runs an unbroken thread, a sense of beauty, strength and continuity of English tradition. Downing Street is its temple and home.

Bibliography

General

Buckle, James Earle (ed), *The Letters of Queen Victoria*, vol. 1, 1930
Hellicar, Eileen, *The Prime Ministers of Great Britain*, 1978
Jameson, Egon, *10 Downing Street*, 1945
Keegan, John, *Who's Who in Military History*, 1976
Lee, Elizabeth, *Wives of the Prime Ministers*, 1918
McLeod, Kirsty, *The Wives of Downing Street*, 1976
Minney, Rubeigh James, *No. 10 Downing Street*, 1963
Petrie, Sir Charles, *The Powers Behind the Prime Ministers*, 1958
Thompson, G. M., *The Prime Ministers*, 1980
Trevelyan, G. M., *English Social History*, 1942
Van Thal, Herbert, *The Prime Ministers*, 2 vols, 1974 & 7
Wilson, Sir Harold, *A Prime Minister on Prime Ministers*, 1977
Wraxall, Sir Nathaniel William, *Historical Memoirs of my Own Time*, 1904

Pitt

Eden, Robert John, 2nd Earl Auckland (ed), *The Journal and Correspondence of William, Lord Auckland*, 1860
Ehrman, John, *The Younger Pitt: the Years of Acclaim*, 1969
Gibson, Edward, Baron Ashbourne, Pitt, *Some Chapters of his Life and Times*, 1898
Primrose, Archibald Philip, 5th Earl Rosebery, *Letters Relating to the Love Episode of William Pitt*, 1900
Reilly, Robin, *Pitt the Younger*, 1978
Stanhope, Philip Henry, 5th Earl, *Life of the Right Honourable William Pitt*, 4 vols, 1861
Tomline, G., *Memoirs of the Life of William Pitt*, 1821

215

Wellington

Arbuthnot, Harriet, *Journal*, vol. 2, 1950
De Grey, Thomas Philip, Earl, *Characteristics of the Duke of Wellington*, 1853
Fraser, Sir William, *Words on Wellington*, 1889
Greville, Charles Cavendish Fulke, *Memoirs*, vol. 6, 1874–87
Guedella, Philip, *The Duke*, 1931
Longford, Elizabeth, *Wellington, Pillar of State*, 1972
Timbs, John, *Wellingtomania*, 1852

Gladstone

Checkland, Sydney George, *The Gladstones*, 1971
Deacon, Richard, *The Private Life of Mr Gladstone*, 1965
Drew, Mary (née Gladstone), *Diaries and Letters*, 1930
Hammond, John L. Le B., *Gladstone and the Irish Nation*, 1938
Marlow, Joyce, *Mr and Mrs Gladstone*, 1977
Morley, John, Viscount, *Life of William Ewart Gladstone*, 1903
Pearsall, Ronald, *The Worm in the Bud*, 1969
Schlüter, Auguste, *A Lady's Maid in Downing Street*, 1922
Somervell, David C., *Disraeli and Gladstone*, 1925

Asquith

Asquith, Margot, Countess of Oxford & Asquith, *Autobiography*, 1920
Haldane, Richard Burdon, Viscount, *Autobiography*, 1929
Holroyd, Michael, *Lytton Strachey*, 1967
Jenkins, Roy, *Mr Balfour's Poodle*, 1954
Jenkins, Roy, *Asquith*, 1964
Jolliffe, John, *Raymond Asquith*, 1980
Koss, Stephen Edward, *Asquith*, 1976
Magnus, Sir Phillip, *King Edward the Seventh*, 1964
Spender, J. A., and Asquith, Cyril, *The Life of Herbert Henry Asquith, Lord Oxford and Asquith*, 2 vols, 1932

Lloyd George

Bowyer, Chaz, *Albert Ball, V.C.*, 1977
Campbell, John, *Lloyd George: The Goat in the Wilderness*, 1977
Davies, Sir Joseph, *The Prime Minister's Secretariat 1916–20*, 1977
George, Richard Lloyd, *Lloyd George*, 1960
George, William, *My Brother and I*, 1958
Hetherington, Sir Hector James Wright, *Life and Letters of Sir Henry Jones*, 1924
Jones, Thomas, CH, *Lloyd George*, 1951
Jones, Thomas, CH, *Whitehall Diary*, 1969
McCormick, Donald, *The Mask of Merlin*, 1963
Owen, Frank, *Tempestuous Journey*, 1954
Riddell, George Allardice, *War Diary, 1914–18*, 1933
Rowland, Peter, *Lloyd George*, 1975
Stevenson, Frances, *Lloyd George: A Diary*, 1971

Ramsay MacDonald

Brockway, Archibald Fenner, *Inside the Left*, 1942
Clynes, John Robert, *Memoirs, 1869–1924*, 1937
Jones, Thomas, CH *Whitehall Diary*, vol. 2, 1969
Marquand, David, *Ramsay MacDonald*, 1977
Nicolson, Sir Harold George, *Diaries & Letters*, vol. 1, 1966
Pelling, Henry Mathison, *The Origins of the Labour Party*, 1965
Sacks, Benjamin, *J. Ramsay MacDonald*, 1952
Snowden, Philip, *Autobiography*, vol. 2, 1934
Taylor, A. J. P., *English History, 1914–45*, 1965
Weir, Lauchlan Macneill, *The Tragedy of Ramsay MacDonald*, 1938

Prime Ministers

Sir Robert Walpole	Whig	1721
Spencer Compton	Whig	1742
Henry Pelham	Whig	1743
Duke of Newcastle	Whig	1754
Duke of Devonshire	Whig	1756
Duke of Newcastle (2)	Whig	1757
Earl of Bute	Tory	1762
George Grenville	Whig	1763
Marquis of Rockingham	Whig	1765
William Pitt (the Elder)	Whig	1766
Duke of Grafton	Whig	1767
Lord North	Tory	1770
Marquis of Rockingham (2)	Whig	1782
Earl of Shelburne	Whig	1782
Duke of Portland	Coalition	1783
William Pitt (the Younger)	Tory	1783
Henry Addington	Tory	1801
William Pitt (the Younger) (2)	Tory	1804
Lord Grenville	Whig	1806
Duke of Portland (2)	Tory	1807
Spencer Perceval	Tory	1809
Lord Liverpool	Tory	1812
George Canning	Tory	1827
Lord Goderich	Tory	1827
Duke of Wellington	Tory	1828
Earl Grey	Whig	1830
Lord Melbourne	Whig	1834
Sir Robert Peel	Tory	1834

Lord Melbourne (2)	Whig	1835
Sir Robert Peel (2)	Tory	1841
Lord John Russell	Whig	1846
Earl of Derby	Conservative	1852
Earl of Aberdeen	Coalition	1852
Viscount Palmerston	Liberal	1855
Earl of Derby (2)	Conservative	1858
Viscount Palmerston (2)	Liberal	1859
Earl (Lord John) Russell (2)	Liberal	1865
Earl of Derby (3)	Conservative	1866
Benjamin Disraeli	Conservative	1868
William Ewart Gladstone	Liberal	1868
Benjamin Disraeli (2)	Conservative	1874
William Ewart Gladstone (2)	Liberal	1880
Marquis of Salisbury	Conservative	1885
William Ewart Gladstone (3)	Liberal	1886
Marquis of Salisbury (2)	Conservative	1886
William Ewart Gladstone (4)	Liberal	1892
Earl of Rosebery	Liberal	1894
Marquis of Salisbury (3)	Conservative	1895
Arthur James Balfour	Conservative	1902
Sir Henry Campbell-Bannerman	Liberal	1905
Herbert Henry Asquith	Liberal	1908
David Lloyd George	Coalition	1916
Andrew Bonar Law	Conservative	1922
Stanley Baldwin	Conservative	1923
James Ramsay MacDonald	Labour	1924
Stanley Baldwin (2)	Conservative	1924
James Ramsay MacDonald (2)	Labour	1929
Stanley Baldwin (3)	National	1935
Neville Chamberlain	National	1937
Sir Winston Churchill	Coalition	1940
Clement Attlee	Labour	1945
Sir Winston Churchill (2)	Conservative	1951
Sir Anthony Eden	Conservative	1955
Harold Macmillan	Conservative	1957
Sir Alec Douglas Home	Conservative	1963
Harold Wilson	Labour	1964
Edward Heath	Conservative	1970
Harold Wilson (2)	Labour	1974
James Callaghan	Labour	1976
Margaret Hilda Thatcher	Conservative	1979

Index

Index

223